Never Let Me Go

Suzanne Heathcote is an award-winning playwright and screenwriter based in the UK and US. Her first play, *Concrete Fairgrounds*, was selected as part of the Royal Court Young Writers Festival. She has since received the New York Stage and Film Founders' Award, was a resident playwright at SPACE on Ryder Farm, and a member of the Ars Nova Play Group, NYC. Other plays include *Plot 10* (Heat & Light Company, Hampstead Theatre), *SO.* (LabRats New York), *I Saw My Neighbor on the Train and I Didn't Even Smile* (New Neighborhood & Berkshire Theatre Group / Redtwist Theatre, Chicago). For screen, Suzanne was lead writer/executive producer for *Killing Eve* (Emmy Award nominee) and writer/executive producer for *The Crowded Room*. Other TV/film credits include *Fear the Walking Dead*, *See*, *Little Voice*, and a rewrite for the upcoming film adaptation of Richard Osman's *The Thursday Murder Club*.

Kazuo Ishiguro was born in Nagasaki, Japan, in 1954 and moved to Britain at the age of five. His works of fiction have earned him many honours around the world, including the Nobel Prize in Literature and the Booker Prize. His books have been translated into over fifty languages. He received a knighthood in 2018 for Services to Literature. He also holds the decorations of Chevalier de l'Ordre des Arts et des Lettres from France and the Order of the Rising Sun, Gold and Silver Star from Japan. His most recent novel, *Klara and the Sun* was a number one *Sunday Times* bestseller in both hardback and paperback.

The Remains of the Day and *Never Let Me Go* were made into acclaimed films. Cinema adaptations of *Klara and the Sun* and of his first novel, *A Pale View of Hills*, will be released in 2025.

Ishiguro also works occasionally as a screenwriter. His screenplay for the 2022 film *Living* received Academy Award (Oscar) and BAFTA nominations.

SUZANNE HEATHCOTE

Never Let Me Go

based on the novel by Kazuo Ishiguro

faber

First published in 2024
by Faber and Faber Limited
The Bindery, 51 Hatton Garden
London, ECIN 8HN

Typeset by Brighton Gray
Printed and bound in the UK by CPI Group (Ltd), Croydon CR0 4YY

All rights reserved
© Suzanne Heathcote, 2024

Suzanne Heathcote is hereby identified as author
of this work in accordance with Section 77 of the
Copyright, Designs and Patents Act 1988

All rights whatsoever in this work, amateur or professional,
are strictly reserved. Applications for permission for any use
whatsoever including performance rights must be made in
advance, prior to any such proposed use,
to Creative Artists Agency, 405 Lexington Avenue,
22nd Floor, New York, NY 10174

No performance may be given unless a licence
has first been obtained

This book is sold subject to the condition that it shall not,
by way of trade or otherwise, be lent, resold, hired out
or otherwise circulated without the publisher's prior consent
in any form of binding or cover other than that in which
it is published and without a similar condition including
this condition being imposed on the subsequent purchaser

A CIP record for this book
is available from the British Library

ISBN 978-0-571-39457-9

Printed and bound in the UK on FSC® certified paper in line with our continuing
commitment to ethical business practices, sustainability and the environment.
For further information see faber.co.uk/environmental-policy

2 4 6 8 10 9 7 5 3 1

Never Let Me Go was commissioned by and first performed at the Rose Theatre, Kingston upon Thames, on 20 September 2024, with the following cast, in alphabetical order:

Hannah / Chrissie / Jessica Amelie Abbott
Miss Emily Susan Aderin
Ruth Matilda Bailes
Kathy Nell Barlow
Phillip / Lenny / Terry Maximus Evans
Tommy Angus Imrie
Laura Princess Khumalo
Miss Lucy / Madame Emilie Patry
Rodney / Alfie Tristan Waterson

Vocals of Judy Bridgewater Marisha Wallace

Additional roles played by members of the company

Director Christopher Haydon
Set & Costume Designer Tom Piper
Movement Director Ayse Tashkiran
Lighting Designer Joshua Carr
Composer Eamonn O'Dwyer
Sound Designer Carolyn Downing
Casting Director Sam Jones CDG
Fight Director Haruka Kuroda
Voice & Dialect Coach Claudette Williams
Assistant Director Emma Denson (Drama League Rose Directing Fellow)

FOR THE ROSE THEATRE
Chief Executive Robert O'Dowd
Artistic Director Christopher Haydon
Executive Producer David Sloan

Never Let Me Go is a Rose Original Production with Bristol Old Vic, Malvern Theatres, and Royal & Derngate, Northampton.

Characters

Kathy
thirty-one, RP accent; nurturing, introverted, observant

Phillip
twenty-three, regional accent; caustic, sensitive, dry

Miss Emily
Head Guardian, sixties, forthright, determined

Tommy
Hailsham student

Ruth
Hailsham student

Hannah
Hailsham student

Laura
Hailsham student

Alfie
Hailsham student

Miss Lucy
thirties; forthright, honest, fair

Madame

Chrissie
seventeen; regional accent, assured, considered, aware

Rodney
seventeen; regional accent, loyal, honest, insecure

Lenny
seventeen; regional accent; confident, genial, perceptive

Jessica
donor

Terry
twenties, carer

Also

Judy Bridgewater (*voice-over*), Nurses, Man, Woman, Administrator, Husband and Wife (*voice-overs*), Possible (*female, thirties*), Doctor, Porters

NEVER LET ME GO

Act One

Darkness.

Within it a song. It's from the mid-1950s. Bossa nova beat. As it plays, light dimly illuminates a woman. Her back to us. Swaying in time to the music.

The song's lyrics emerge through the female singer's voice. Her singing is haunting. Sensual. Something akin to 'You're My Thrill' by Dolores Gray. But this isn't Dolores Gray.

This is Judy Bridgewater.

Judy Bridgewater   (*Voice-over; singing.*)
   Oh baby, baby.

>   *The woman swaying to the music slowly turns. She is holding a pillow. Cradling it like a baby in her arms. Eyes closed. She sings along with Judy:*

Judy Bridgewater *and* **Woman**   (*Singing.*)
   Oh baby, baby.
   Oh baby, baby.
   Never let me –

Phillip   I thought this was my room.

SCENE ONE: THE ROOM

The woman, Kathy, is next to a bed plumping a pillow in a room which is clinical. Clean. Impersonal.

Kathy   It is.

>   *At the door stands Phillip. He's wearing an overcoat. A duffel bag over his shoulder.*

(Re: the pillow.) Sorry I was just checking they'd.

They can be a bit lax here so I.

A projection: 'PART ONE: ENGLAND, 1998'.

It's Phillip isn't it?

I'm Kathy. Kathy H.

Your carer.

Phillip looks at the bed.

Phillip Can I –

Kathy Yes. Yes of course.

They switch places. Phillip sets his bag on the bed. He begins unpacking his things. Some pyjamas. Underwear. A toothbrush. He puts them in a small cupboard.

Was the journey long?

Phillip Couple of hours.

Kathy Oh not too bad then.

Well you don't have any appointments today so you can just relax. Settle in.

I can give you a tour of the centre if you like?

Phillip continues unpacking.

You're lucky. It's nice here.

Phillip Nice and lax?

You said they can be a bit lax.

Kathy Oh. Not with anything. Important.

Is there anything you'd like me to bring on my visits?

Fruit juice?

Biscuits?

Novels –

Phillip *Novels?*

Kathy Yes. If there's a particular author you like or.

I pass a second-hand bookshop on the way so –

Phillip How often will you be here?

Kathy Couple of times a week.

More around the time of your first.

Phillip continues unpacking.

You must have been a carer?

Phillip Not for long.

Told them I wanted to get on with it.

Kathy Well that's very.

Good for you.

I've been doing it eleven years now.

Phillip *Eleven?*

Kathy It'll be twelve in January.

Phillip Bloody hell. You must be the world's best carer.

Kathy Well I know someone who did it for fourteen and she was pretty useless so.

I wouldn't get your hopes up.

Kathy smiles. Phillip doesn't.

Phillip Aren't you bored shitless? With all the travelling and appointments and.

People.

Kathy	I like the travelling. And the people.
Phillip	But it's such a waste of time.
Kathy	How do you mean?
Phillip	Well it's not what we're here for is it?
	It's not what we're supposed to be doing.
Kathy	I think it's all part of it. Making someone's experience.
	Better.
Phillip	Are you going to make my experience better?
Kathy	I hope so.
	Phillip looks at Kathy.
	Kathy looks at Phillip.
	Phillip goes back to unpacking.
Phillip	Pick-and-mix.
	I like pick-and-mix.
Kathy	Alright. That's easy enough.
	Kathy takes out a small notebook and makes a note.
Phillip	But not Refreshers. I hate them.
	They get stuck in my teeth.
Kathy	No Refreshers. Got it.
	Phillip organises his things in the cupboard.
	Right.
	Well.
	I should go and chat to them out there. Get your appointment schedule and –

Phillip	Did you go to Hailsham?
	Kathy stops. At the word 'Hailsham', there's a low, almost imperceptible hum.
Kathy	What makes you say that?
Phillip	You just seem so.
	Hailsham.
	The hum *gets louder.*
Kathy	Have you met many Hailsham students?
Phillip	None.
	But I've heard things.
	I'm right aren't I?
	You were a Hailsham kid.
	The hum *gets louder.*
	Bloody hell.
	Didn't it close down years ago?
	You must be one of the last ones left.
	The hum *gets louder.*
Kathy	Nice meeting you Phillip.
	I'll make sure to bring you that pick-and –
Phillip	How does the man on the moon cut his hair?

SCENE TWO: THE ROOM

Phillip is sitting on the bed, clothed. He's eating sweets from a bag of pick-and-mix.

Kathy sits on a chair across from him. She's filling in various forms.

Phillip Eclipse it.

The room has signs of being lived in. The weather outside different. The light of day altered.

Kathy (*Reading.*) Night sweats?

Phillip What did the sea say to the beach?

Kathy Shortness of breath?

Phillip Nothing. It just waved.

Kathy Blurred vision? Floaters?

Phillip What's brown and sticky?

Kathy Phillip please.

Phillip A stick.

Phillip looks at the sweets in the bag. Takes one out.

They're going to ask all those questions when we're in there.

Kathy Well they ask for the forms beforehand. So we give them the forms.

Phillip When I was a carer I let people fill out the forms for themselves.

Like grown-ups.

Kathy Maybe that's why you weren't a carer very long.

Phillip eats the sweet.

(*Reading.*) How many times have you urinated in the last twenty-four hours?

Phillip Two cannibals are eating a clown.

Kathy slams her pen down.

One says to the other 'Does this taste funny to you?'

I saw a hint of a smile at that one.

Kathy (*Holding out the forms.*) Okay fine. Do them yourself.

Phillip looks at the forms. Looks at them.

Goes back to his sweets.

Phillip I've urinated approximately five or six times in the last twenty-four hours.

Kathy Thank you.

Kathy goes back to the forms.

Any headaches?

Phillip indicates no. Kathy marks the form.

Numbness or tingling in your hands or feet?

Phillip indicates no. Kathy marks the form.

Alright I just need to check this. And you'll be happy to know we're done.

She walks over to Phillip and takes his temperature. Phillip focuses on the ceiling.

What did the pirate say on his eightieth birthday?

'Aye matey.'

Phillip looks at Kathy. Unsmiling.

Yours weren't any better.

She takes the thermometer out of his mouth. Walks to her notebook. Makes a note.

Phillip They're not supposed to be.

They're from this book. *A Thousand-and-One Bad Jokes.*

Kathy And you remember the worst of them do you?

Phillip I remember them all.

Kathy A thousand-and-one? Do you have a photographic memory?

Phillip One of the boys would read from it every night in our dorm.

You hear anything enough times. Eventually it goes in.

Kathy You must have been bored sick of it.

Phillip It was the only book we had so.

Phillip goes back to his sweets.

Kathy fills out the form. Stops.

Looks at Phillip.

Kathy You didn't have anything else to read?

Phillip indicates no.

What about English lessons?

Phillip A few textbooks.

Kathy You didn't read any novels?

Phillip No. We didn't read any – (*Imitating her.*) 'novels'.

Kathy	That's terrible.
Phillip	*That's terrible.* God you don't half lay it on thick do you.
Kathy	No I just mean. Books. Stories. They can.
They take you other places.
Phillip	Maybe I don't want to go other places.
Kathy	I could bring you some of my favourites –
Phillip	You're alright thanks.
Kathy	Honestly it's no trouble. A good book would really help pass the –
Phillip	There's no fucking point.
My reading's shite.
Kathy looks at Phillip. Then:
Kathy	I could read *to* you –
Phillip	Piss off. I'm not a child.
Kathy	No that wasn't what I.
No.
Kathy goes back to the forms.
Phillip looks at his sweets.
Eats one.
Phillip	So it's true what they say about Hailsham then?
A low hum.
Kathy remains focused on the forms.
Kathy	I've no idea what they say.
Phillip	Oh come on. You must know.
Hailsham's *legendary*.

The hum *gets louder.*

I tell you what. I'd rather hear about Hailsham than some crappy old book.

The hum *gets louder.*

Were you one of the ones to get a deferral?

Is that why you're still doing this?

Kathy continues working on the forms.

It's funny. You get this look.

This expression. Every time I mention it.

'Hailsham.'

The hum *gets louder.*

It's like you're.

Scared.

Kathy (*Slamming her file closed.*) Enough!

Phillip What?

Kathy I've had enough. Of you Phillip.

I've had enough of you.

Kathy starts packing her things away.

Phillip I don't understand –

Kathy Everything's a battle. Filling out your forms. Taking your vitals. Finding ways to occupy you –

Phillip Is this because I don't read –

Kathy This isn't working. You need a different carer.

Phillip What? No!

Look I know I'm a bit of a prick sometimes. But changing carer won't help.

I'm like it with everyone.

Kathy stands with her back to Phillip, closes her eyes.

I'm sorry. I didn't think it would upset you.

About Hailsham.

I won't mention it again I promise.

Kathy?

The way people talk about it. I'd assumed Hailsham was amazing.

That your memories were good.

Kathy They are. But I don't like to.

They are.

Phillip The thing is.

You have all this time to prepare for being in here.

But it's only once you are that you realise.

All you have to think about. Are the things in your head.

And I don't like what's in my head.

Kathy looks at Phillip.

Looks at Phillip.

She puts down the paperwork.

Kathy Alright. You can ask me one question.

One question about Hailsham. And then we're done.

Phillip One?

Kathy One.

He sits back. Thinks.

Phillip Was it.

No.

What was your.

No hang on.

Okay.

What was Hailsham like?

Kathy laughs.

Kathy That's a bit broad.

Phillip Well give me a description of the place. Detailed though. Not just some 'it looked nice' bollocks.

Kathy Alright.

(*Thinking.*) Alright.

The Hailsham property was in the middle of the countryside. With nothing else around for miles.

As Kathy describes Hailsham, it appears. Surrounding them.

Being that secluded made it feel like we were living in our own little world. But it also meant that when we finally came to leave.

Leaving was a shock.

Anyway. There was the main house. Where we had all our lessons.

Miss Emily Quieten down please. Quieten down!

A class of students (aged ten) are being taught by Miss Emily. She's taking them through the towns in Oxfordshire, as 1970s pictures of the locations appear as part of a slideshow.

Kathy It was an old historic building. Pretty unforgiving.

Miss Emily Hannah P. Don't think I can't see you playing noughts and crosses with Laura J.

Kathy Freezing in the winter. Boiling in the summer.

Miss Emily Now where were we? Ah yes.

Miss Emily looks to the slide.

Chipping Norton.

Kathy But from the outside it looked quite impressive. Like an old stately home.

A new slide image appears.

Miss Emily Burford.

Kathy Miss Emily was the Head Guardian of Hailsham.

The slides progress as Kathy walks Phillip through the classroom.

Miss Emily Witney.

Kathy She was strict. But fair.

Miss Emily And Oxford.

Kathy Very no-nonsense.

Miss Emily And that completes Oxfordshire.

Where shall we go next?

Kathy But the students respected her. Revered her even you could say.

The slide changes to show a map of Great Britain.

Miss Emily Now over here. We've got Norfolk. Which is a lovely part of the country.

Very charming. Because it's not on the way to anywhere.

People bypass it you see.

Making Norfolk something of. A lost corner.

Tommy raises his hand.

Yes Tommy.

Tommy So does all our lost property go to Norfolk?

The students laugh.

Kathy looks at Tommy.

Kathy Afterwards we referred to anything we lost as having 'gone to Norfolk'.

Tommy looks at Kathy. Smiles.

Kathy smiles at Tommy.

Phillip Was the main building just for lessons then?

Kathy (*Snapping back.*) No. We'd have lunch in the main hall.

And assembly every morning.

No wait. Assembly was just Mondays Wednesdays and Fridays I think.

Yes that's right.

But we had the Exchanges and Sales in the main house.

Phillip Exchanges and Sales?

Kathy Didn't you have those where you were?

Phillip indicates no.

	The Exchanges were like a sort of. Art fair that was held every term.
	The students appear with their 'work' presented on tables.
	We'd each put our work on display for the other students.
Phillip	What do you mean *work*?
Kathy	Drawings. Paintings. Poetry. Short stories. Anything deemed *artistic*. We'd buy and sell it to each other with our tokens which we'd been saving all term.
	Kathy picks up one of the drawings on display. Looks at it.
	It seems bonkers now. But we'd fight over one of Tamara D's pond paintings. Or Marjorie P's papier-mâché giraffes. We valued it all enormously. At least.
	We valued the things that were in great demand.
Phillip	I bet your stuff was in great demand.
Kathy	My stuff was decidedly average.
	Looking back I suppose the Exchanges were good in many ways. We came to appreciate each other's art. And it gave us something to strive for. To have other students buying your work made you feel. Accomplished.
Ruth	The problem is she overcharges.
Kathy	But it also meant our art became a kind of. Currency.
	Ruth, Hannah and Laura (aged eleven) are looking at some of the work on display.

Ruth	No one's going to pay four tokens for that when it could get you one of my boat paintings instead.
Kathy	Those who were good at being creative were held in very high esteem. And those who weren't –
Ruth	Tommy what are you doing?
	Tommy is displaying his paintings on a table.
Kathy	It could be very hard for the ones who weren't.
	Alfie (aged eleven) has also appeared.
Tommy	What does it look like?
Hannah	You don't actually think you're going to sell any of these do you?
Laura	They look like they've been painted by a two-year-old.
Alfie	That's because he is a two-year-old. (*Indicating his brain.*) Up here.
	Alfie throws Tommy's paintings into the air and the students walk away, laughing.
Tommy	Piss off Alfie! You. Arse!
	Tommy looks down at his work scattered on the floor.
	Kathy starts to pick the paintings up.
	Don't. Leave it.
	It doesn't matter. They're rubbish anyway.
	Tommy kicks the paintings and walks away.
Kathy	(*Calling after him.*) I don't think they're rubbish.

(Looking at a painting.) I like them.

Tommy is gone.

Phillip And the Sales were something different?

Kathy The Sales were different entirely.

The Exchanges were quiet. Solemn. Reverential even.

The Sales were like a big raucous jumble sale.

The students bring cardboard boxes into the space.

There'd be a delivery of boxes a few times a year containing things from the outside. And the next day everything would be laid out in the main hall ready for us to buy what we wanted with our tokens.

The students begin to rummage through the boxes.

Phillip What kind of stuff would there be?

Kathy Oh it was absolute tat mostly.

Broken toys.

Half-used pens.

Board games with missing pieces.

The students are fighting over the items as they're mentioned.

But we didn't care. To us anything from the outside was exotic.

And occasionally you'd find some little piece of treasure.

Ruth A pencil case!

Tommy	A polo shirt!
Laura	A fully functioning Etch-A-Sketch!
	The students immediately tussle with Laura for the Etch-A-Sketch.
Kathy	So there was always the hope.
	The possibility.
	That the next Sale would have something special in it. Waiting just for you.
Phillip	What was the best bit of treasure you got?
Kathy	The best thing I ever bought. The thing I loved most.
	Was a cassette tape. An album.
	Songs After Dark by Judy Bridgewater.
Phillip	Never heard of her.
Kathy	She was an American lounge singer from the fifties. It was very old-fashioned.
	But there was this one song I absolutely adored.
	The song begins to play.
	I played it over and over.
	Until the tape got lost.
	Kathy gets caught in the music for a moment.
	She then turns away and the music suddenly stops.
	To the left of the main house. No wait. To the *right*. Was the playing field.
	The students are doing jumping jacks with Miss Lucy.

	That's where we'd have PE.
Miss Lucy	Five. Six. Seven. Eight. Keep it up Alfie D.
	Jumping jacks for jollity.
Alfie	(*Breathless.*) Yes. Miss. Lucy.
	Miss Lucy blows a whistle as she leads the class in a jog around the space.
Kathy	And then behind the playing field were the dorm buildings.
	One for the girls and one for the boys.
	The female students lie down as if in beds. Hannah holds a torch under her face.
Hannah	When suddenly. There was a tap. Tap. Tap at the window.
Kathy	I remember when we were about eleven. My dorm was constantly getting into trouble for scaring each other witless with ghost stories after lights out.
Hannah	Tap. Tap. Tap. But there was no one *at* the window.
Kathy	I don't know why we got so scared because the story was always the same. It was about a student from Hailsham years before our time. Who'd snuck out one day to explore the woods to the back of the grounds.
Hannah	When from the silence. A voice could be heard.
Kathy	But as soon as she was out of Hailsham. She couldn't find her way back in. So she roamed the woods all alone until she died.
Laura	(*Covering her ears.*) Please. Stop. I won't be able to sleep!

Kathy	They said if you were very quiet. You could hear her ghost. Crying out –

Hannah	Let me back in.	**Kathy**	Let me back in.
	Please!		Please!
	LET ME BACK IN.		LET ME BACK IN.

The students scream and run out of the room. Except Ruth. Who starts brushing her hair.

Kathy sits and watches Ruth.

Watches her.

Kathy	You know. I used to read to Ruth.
	All the time when we were older.
	And it never made her feel like a child.
Phillip	Who's Ruth?

Ruth disappears. Kathy turning to Phillip in –

SCENE THREE: A WAITING ROOM

Phillip is sitting next to Kathy within a row of chairs against the wall.

Phillip	Was she your best friend?
Kathy	Hang on. Didn't we say one question?
Phillip	It's not a question about *Hailsham*. We're just chatting about old friends.
	My best friend Jeremy used to do this thing where he'd turn his eyelids inside out and go up to the girls and talk to them. Like he was totally normal. And they'd all scream and run away.

It was brilliant.

He looks to her, asking in a stilted 'non Hailsham question' way –

Who were *your* best friends Kathy?

Kathy narrows her eyes at Phillip. Tries to conceal a smile.

I bet you had loads of friends. Loads of friends to lounge around with.

Reading *novels*.

Kathy It wasn't a holiday camp you know.

And loads is probably a bit.

I had a small group who I.

Two in particular that I –

Ruth Do you want to ride one of my horses?

Ruth (aged six) trots around the space on a 'horse'. Hannah and Laura skipping together. Tommy playing alone with some building blocks.

Kathy And yes. Ruth was one of them.

Ruth I've got Bramble. And Clover. And Flossie.

Kathy She was my first friend at Hailsham.

Ruth There's also Thunder but you can't ride him because he'd be too dangerous so only I can ride Thunder.

Kathy One of my earliest memories is of us in the infants. Playing together outside.

Ruth But you have to swear not to use a crop on them.

Kathy	She was forceful. Defiant. Even then.
Ruth	If you use a crop you're banned.
Kathy	I really looked up to her. The way she'd hold her ground. And insist on what she wanted.
Ruth	BLOODY WELL PICK ONE THEN!
Kathy	Clover. I'll take Clover.
Ruth	Clover. Good choice.

Ruth hands the reins over to Kathy, and they both start to trot around the space.

They trot faster and faster, round and round. Both laughing with the game when –

Hannah	Kathy what are you doing?
Kathy	Playing horses.

Hannah and Laura laugh.

Hannah	That's so babyish.
Kathy	No it's not.
Hannah	Playing horses is a baby's game Kathy. Everyone knows that.

Don't they Ruth?

Kathy turns to Ruth.

Ruth says nothing.

Kathy But for all Ruth's defiance. For all her strength.

Hannah and Laura walk away.

The thing she was most aware of. I think maybe more than anything.

Was how other people saw her.

Kathy turns to Ruth.

	I don't care what they say.
	I like the horses.
	Kathy starts trotting on her horse.
Ruth	Don't do that.
	It's babyish.
Kathy	It was like she had this. Sense.
	Of how she was being perceived.
Ruth	She's frightened of us.
	Ruth Laura and Hannah (eleven) are sitting at their desks, talking together.
Kathy	Not that it made her any less commanding.
Hannah	She can't be frightened of us. We're only children!
Kathy	Ruth never let anyone get in the way of her opinions.
Ruth	I've seen the way she looks at us and I'm telling you.
Kathy	When we were about eleven. She had this theory about one of the guardians.
Ruth	She's frightened of us.
Kathy	I say guardian. She wasn't really a guardian.
	Come to think of it we didn't even know her name. She was just.
	'Madame.'
	Madame appears. Wearing a grey skirt suit. Clutching an attaché case.
	She was either French or Belgian. I never quite knew which.

Everything about her was a mystery to us. We always knew she was coming to Hailsham. Because the day before the guardians would take all our best artwork and lay it out in the billiard room.

Madame would arrive the next day. And without saying a word to anyone. Lock herself in that room. Poring over our art with a kind of.

Quiet intensity.

Madame looks at a table covered in pictures. Slowly picking one up after another.

At the end of the day she'd choose a few select pieces. Put them in her case.

And take them with her.

Madame puts some paintings into her attaché case.

And we wouldn't see her until the next mysterious visit. Where she'd do exactly the same thing again.

Phillip   Where was she taking the art?

Kathy   The rumour among the students was that she took it to a gallery in Paris where our work was being exhibited. Ridiculous really. But it was a source of great pride. Having Madame select your work for the *Gallery*.

Phillip   Did no one ever ask?

Kathy   We just felt not to.

Whenever Madame was mentioned by one of the guardians. It was with hushed tones and serious expressions. The whole topic felt out of bounds.

Although something did come up once with Miss Emily –

Miss Emily is teaching the students. Alfie raises his hand.

Alfie Miss.

Kathy There'd been this feeling among the students at the time. That we should be compensated for the work that was taken by Madame.

Miss Emily nods to him.

Alfie When Madame takes our best artwork. We don't have those things to sell at the Exchanges.

Miss Emily That's the price you pay for being talented Alfie.

Alfie But shouldn't we at least get some tokens for what she takes?

Miss Emily If your work is chosen by Madame. It's a great honour.

And that is payment enough.

Hannah raises her hand.

Hannah Does Madame take our art to a gallery?

Silence. Everyone looks at Miss Emily.

Miss Emily Well.

Yes. It is a sort of gallery.

In a way.

It's very hard to explain. And when you're older.

When you have a better grasp of things.

You might come to understand.

But for now all you need to know. Is your work is taken somewhere that's.

Very. Very. Important.

Because.

Lights on Tommy. Watching Miss Emily.

Well because. Your artwork.

Lights on Kathy. Watching Tommy.

Gives people a glimpse.

Lights on Ruth. Watching Kathy.

Into your souls.

The students all stand as –

Kathy I've lost my train. Where was I?

Phillip Ruth and Madame. Being frightened of you.

Ruth She is!

Kathy Oh yes. Ruth was convinced Madame was frightened of us.

Ruth Laura and Hannah are gathered.

Hannah I think she's just snooty.

Ruth I used to think that too. But it's something else.

The way she looks at us. It's like.

We're spiders or something.

I can prove it if you want.

Laura How can you prove a thing like that?

Ruth She's in the billiard room right now.

When she comes out. Let's swarm around her.

And as we do. Watch her face.

Hannah She's coming!

Ruth	Watch her face.
	Madame, carrying her attaché case, exits the billiard room.
	Ruth indicates 'go', and the girls surround Madame in a close circle.
	Madame raises her hands so as not to be touched by them.
Madame	What are you doing?
	Her face holding an expression of horror.
	Get away from me.
	GET AWAY!
	Madame pushes past the girls and runs off.
Hannah	If she doesn't like us. Why does she want our work?
	Why doesn't she just leave us alone?
	WHO ASKED HER TO BLOODY WELL COME HERE ANYWAY?!
	Hannah and Laura disappear as Kathy and Ruth remain, looking into the distance.
Kathy	You were right.
Ruth	I don't want to be right Kath.
	I just wanted you to see it.
Kathy	She's terrified of us.
	Why? What did we do?
Ruth	I just wanted you to see it Kath.
	So you'd feel it with me.
	So you'd feel it with me too.

	Kathy turns to Ruth. Looks at her. Looks.
Phillip	You said there were two.
	Kathy snaps out of the memory, and Ruth disappears.
	Two people. You were best friends with.
	Who was the other?
	Kathy considers.
	Considers.
Kathy	Did you ever have someone. That you were just.
	Aware of?
	Somebody you. Noticed.
	Quietly.
	In ways other people didn't?
Phillip	Yes.
Kathy	That's how it was with Tommy.
	Tommy appears (twelve). He's holding a football under one arm.
	I can't remember when I became conscious of Tommy.
	He was always just. There. In the periphery.
	I'd see him and I'd know somehow.
	Understand.
	How he would be feeling.
Tommy	Guys! Over here.
	Kathy looks at Tommy.
Kathy	Almost before he did.

Tommy	Alfie mate.
Kathy	But we didn't start talking properly till I was about twelve.
Tommy	Here!
Ruth	Oh God. What's he doing now.

Ruth Laura and Hannah (twelve) are sitting on the grass. The sound and light of summer surrounds them. They watch Tommy, as if from a distance.

Tommy	Alfie! Harry!
Kathy	Tommy's wearing his favourite shirt.
Laura	Look at him! Totally convinced he's going to be first pick.
Kathy	His favourite polo shirt.
Laura	He has to know they're winding him up.
Tommy	Alfie mate! Come on!
Kathy	It's the blue polo shirt that he got in the Sales.
Hannah	(*Shouting through her hands.*) They're never going to choose you. You fool.
Kathy	He's going to get mud all over it.
Tommy	(*To the unseen boys.*) Well thanks a lot. CRETINS!

Tommy throws the football down. Kicks the grass.

Laura	Oh. Wait for it. Here it comes.

Tommy balls his fists. Holds his breath.

Ruth	Countdown!

Hannah	Six. Five. Four –
Laura	I can barely watch!

Tommy starts stamping his feet. Faster and faster.

Hannah	Three. Two –
Tommy	AAAAAAAAAAAAAAAAAAAAAAAAA!

Tommy bellows from the pit of his stomach. Full volume. His arms and legs flailing. Like a child throwing a full-body tantrum.

The girls roar with laughter. Except Kathy.

STUPID BLOODY BUGGERING ARSE BALLS PISS SHIT DICKS BLOODY FUCKING TOSSING SHITS –

Kathy Tommy.

Kathy is now standing beside Tommy.

Tommy AAAAAHHHH HHHHHHHH HHHHHHHH AAAAAHHHH HHHHHHHH HHHHHHHH!

Kathy Tommy your shirt.

Your nice shirt.

You're going to ruin it.

Kathy puts her hand on Tommy's arm when at the same moment he raises it, accidentally striking her across the face.

Gasps from the girls.

Kathy and Tommy are still.

Still.

Kathy Your shirt Tommy. You've got mud all over your shirt.

Tommy looks down at his shirt and cries out in horror.

Don't worry.

If you take it to Miss Jody she can clean it for you.

Tommy looks at Kathy.

Kathy looks at Tommy.

Tommy runs away.

Phillip   Why would he go bonkers like that?

The girls disappear.

Kathy   I don't know. It was just.

Something he did.

Phillip   And you still liked him?

Kathy laughs.

Kathy   Well he didn't act like that all the time. It was just a phase.

He calmed down as he got older.

And became happier.

Popular even.

Tommy   Kathy.

Tommy appears at the duck pond.

Kathy   In fact it wasn't long after that day on the field.

That things started to change for him.

Tommy   Kath.

Kathy   Which was around the time we started talking.

Tommy   I wanted to say sorry. About what happened.

Kathy	I don't think either of us thought we'd become close or anything.
Tommy	I honestly didn't mean to hit you.
Kathy	But we were just. At ease with each another. Right from the start.
Tommy	I wouldn't dream of hitting a girl.
Kathy	It's okay Tommy. An accident is all.
Tommy	It didn't hurt did it?
Kathy	Sure. Fractured skull. Concussion the lot.
	It's one hundred per cent forgotten.
Tommy	Thanks Kathy. I've been worrying about it ever since it happened.
	Kathy looks at Tommy.
Kathy	I noticed you didn't lose your temper with the boys in PE the other day.
Tommy	You notice everything don't you Kath?
Kathy	You know if you always kept your cool like that. They'd leave you alone.
Tommy	Yeah. That's what I've been thinking.
	I just need to keep my head down. Not let it bother me so much.
	Kathy looks at Tommy.
Kathy	What's happened to you Tommy?
Tommy	(*Laughing.*) What do you mean?
Kathy	You seem. Different.
Tommy	(*Laughing.*) You're a nosy one aren't you Kath?

	Alright. If you must know something has happened.
	Something that's helped the way I think about things.
Kathy	Go on.
Tommy	It was a few weeks ago. We were leaving Art Appreciation when Miss Lucy told me to wait back at the end. I was half expecting her to give me another lecture about how I should try harder with my art. But she didn't say anything like that all. She just turned to me and said –
Miss Lucy	I've known a lot of students who've found it difficult to be creative.
	Miss Lucy appears. Tommy and Kathy looking at her.
	Painting. Drawing. Poetry. But ultimately.
	Ultimately.
	If you've genuinely tried. If you've tried but you're not very creative. That's quite alright. Do you hear?
	You mustn't worry about it. It doesn't matter if you don't sell your things at the Exchanges. Or Madame doesn't select your work.
	It's simply not your fault.
Kathy	She wasn't having you on was she? It wasn't a clever way of telling you off?
Tommy	It definitely wasn't anything like that. It was as if she was angry. But not angry at me.
Miss Lucy	You're not being taught enough. Not nearly enough.

	I've a good mind to talk to you all about it myself.
Kathy	She thinks we should be studying harder than we already are?!
Tommy	No. She was talking about. You know.
	Us.
	What's going to happen to us. Donations and all of that.
Kathy	But we *have* been taught about that.
Tommy	Maybe I got it wrong Kath. I don't know.
	Funny thing is. It did help. What she said. It helped a lot. Because afterwards. Thinking about it. I realised she was right. It isn't my fault. Not being creative.
	And sometimes when I'm feeling a bit rocky about it. I catch her eye.
	Tommy looks at Miss Lucy. Miss Lucy looks at Tommy.
	And she gives me a little nod.
	Miss Lucy looks up and says –
Nurse 1	Phillip R?
	Miss Lucy becomes the Nurse, reading from a clipboard in the Waiting Room.
Phillip	Yes.
Nurse 1	(*Off the clipboard.*) This way please.
Kathy	I'll wait here.
	Phillip exits with the Nurse.
	Kathy looks out. Tommy still next to her.

Tommy You won't tell anyone will you? About what Miss Lucy said.

Ruth appears the other side of the space. Observing Kathy and Tommy.

I haven't told anyone Kath.

Only you.

Kathy I won't say a word Tommy.

Tommy You promise?

Tommy holds out his little finger. Kathy links it with hers.

They look at one another.

Ruth watches Tommy and Kathy.

See you round Kath.

Kathy See you Tommy.

Tommy starts to exit. As he starts to walk away, he does a little run while saying:

Tommy Splash splash splash.

Kathy What's that Tommy?

He stops. Turns to Kathy. Smiles.

Tommy runs a little more.

Tommy Splash splash spl—

Ruth Kathy what are you doing here?

Tommy stops. Kathy spins around to Ruth.

With him?

Tommy Nothing. I was just. I'm going.

(*Exiting.*) See you Kath.

Kathy nods to Tommy. He exits.

Ruth   I don't know why you'd give him the time of day.

Kathy   He's alright.

Ruth   He's a lunatic. He hit you.

Kathy   It was an accident.

Ruth   According to him.

Anyway I've been looking for you all over.

I wanted to give you something.

Ruth holds out a small paper bag for Kathy.

It's from yesterday's Sale.

I got it for you.

Kathy   Ruth. You didn't need to do that.

Ruth   I wanted to.

Ever since you lost that tape you loved.

Kathy   *Songs After Dark?*

Ruth   I've been trying to find a replacement for you.

Kathy suddenly beams as she rushes to take the item out of the bag. It's a cassette tape.

'Twenty Classic Dance Tunes'. *Kathy's smile falters.*

I know it's not the same one.

But I thought it might be a good substitute.

The smile then restores.

Kathy   It's a lovely substitute.

Thank you Ruth.

Thank you so much.

Ruth	I know how sad you were.
	When your tape went to Norfolk.
	And when I saw that at the Sale I thought.
	Kath's my best friend. So I'm going to get her this.
	Because that's what best friends do.
	They look out for each other. First and foremost.

Kathy looks at the tape. Then look up at Ruth. She is about to speak as –

The sound of cars passing.

SCENE FOUR: A PETROL STATION

A Man and Woman stand behind the till. They wear uniforms and name badges.

Kathy's looking at the magazines on the shelves.

Man	She said she needed to think about it.
Kathy	Excuse me.
Woman	Stupid bitch –
Kathy	Excuse me sir.
Man	I expected as much.
Kathy	Please could you point me in the direction of the quiz books?

The Man and Woman look at Kathy.

They look at Kathy.

Look.

Something with visual quizzes would be ideal.

Spot the difference. Mazes.

That kind of thing.

The Man points to where the quiz books are.

Thank you.

The Man and the Woman continue staring at Kathy.

Kathy picks up a quiz book and puts it on the counter.

That. And pump number six please.

The Woman rings it up on the till.

The Man stares at Kathy.

Woman Eighteen forty-six.

Kathy gives the woman some cash.

The Woman gives Kathy some change.

The Man stares at Kathy.

Kathy Thank you.

Kathy takes her things. Exits.

They watch her go.

Watch her go.

Man She's one of them.

Woman Yeah.

God.

The Woman shudders.

Gives me the creeps.

The Man and Woman disappear as Kathy gets into her car.

She flicks through the quiz book.

Ruth Have you finished the exercise on how to buy food shopping?

Ruth (twelve) is sitting next to Kathy.

Kathy (*Still focused on the book.*) Yes.

Ruth Can I have a look?

Kathy nods.

I find these ones really hard. Remembering what products belong where and all of that.

Kathy It's because they've made it out like a test. Once we're outside and actually doing it. We'll learn it all fast enough.

Ruth You know that book Miss Emily uses. With that chapter on 'urban spaces'.

There's this picture of an office. It's a big room with lots of desks lined up in rows. And people in suits are standing around talking. Or sitting typing. Or making calls on the phone.

That's what I'd like to do. When I'm older.

Kathy What do you mean?

Ruth I'd like to be an office lady.

Like the ones in the picture.

Maybe that's what my possible is.

An office lady.

Maybe that's why I want to do it so much.

Kathy looks at Ruth.

41

	You won't tell anyone will you?
Kathy	No.
Ruth	You mean it Kath? You promise?

They link their little fingers to seal the promise. Kathy closes her eyes.

She opens them. Ruth is gone.

Phillip	Is that what you called them? Possibles?

SCENE FIVE: AN EXAMINATION ROOM

Phillip and Kathy sit on a bed next to one another. Waiting.

Kathy	Yes. What did you call them?
Phillip	Others.
Kathy	Others?
Phillip	Yeah. The person you came from was your other. As in. 'I bet your other was thick as shit.' Kind of thing.
Kathy	Is that what they'd say where you were?
Phillip	That's the good version.
Kathy	We never spoke about our possibles much at Hailsham. The guardians shut down any talk around it at all.
	Secretly you'd think. Imagine. Who your possible was.
	But it was something you'd only share with the closest person to you.
	It's funny.
	I thought I'd forgotten most of this stuff.

But all this time it's just been. Sitting there. Waiting.

Kathy looks at her watch.

Shouldn't be much longer.

Phillip bites his lip.

It's just a few scans. Nothing to worry about.

Phillip nods.

Bites his lip.

Phillip What if I complete. After my first?

Kathy You won't.

Phillip How do you know?

Kathy Because no one completes after their first.

Phillip How do you *know*?

Kathy Well I've been doing this for eleven years and I've never seen it.

She takes a puzzle book out of her bag. Holds it out to Phillip.

I noticed you'd finished the last one.

Phillip looks at the book.

Looks at it.

Phillip Did you know.

Among the art and the poems –

Kathy And the novels.

Phillip The fucking novels.

Did you know what was waiting for you when you left?

Kathy We'd been told from the beginning. Who we were and.

We'd had classes preparing us for certain things. Along with all the talk of health that I'm sure you had too. The terror around cigarettes and alcohol and all of that.

But when I think about what I expected life to be. After Hailsham.

I see now. That I didn't know anything.

What about you?

Phillip We knew nothing else.

Kathy I realise Hailsham must sound idyllic. But I found out years later that it received a lot of criticism. People felt we weren't being prepared properly for what lay ahead.

Miss Lucy No. No. I'm sorry. I'm going to have to interrupt you.

Miss Lucy appears. Along with the sound of rain.

You must forgive me for listening but I couldn't help it.

Alfie why don't you tell the others what you were saying just now?

The students (aged fifteen) are crowded together as if taking shelter from the rain. One of them holding a cricket bat and ball.

Go on Alfie. Please tell the others what you were saying.

Alfie We were just talking about what it would feel like if we became actors.

What sort of life it would be.

Miss Lucy Yes. And you were saying you'd have to go to America.

Alfie Yes Miss Lucy.

Miss Lucy looks at the rest of the class.

Miss Lucy I know you don't mean any harm but there's just too much talk like this. I hear it all the time. It's been allowed to go on and it's not right.

The problem is you've been told and not told.

You've been told. But none of you really understand. And I dare say some people are quite happy to leave it that way. But I'm not.

None of you will go to America.

None of you will be film stars.

And none of you will be working in supermarkets as I heard some of you planning the other day.

Your lives are set out for you.

You'll become adults. Then before you're old. Before you're even middle-aged.

You'll start to donate your vital organs.

That's what you were created to do.

You were each of you cloned for that exact purpose.

You're not like the actors you see on videos. You're not even like me.

You were brought into this world for a purpose. And your futures. All of them. Have been decided.

So you're not to talk that way any more.

You'll be leaving Hailsham very soon. And it's not so far off. The day you'll be preparing for your first donations.

And if you're to have decent lives. You have to know who you are and what lies ahead of you. Every one of you.

The students are still.

Still.

The rain's not so bad now. Let's just go out there.

And maybe the sun will come out.

Miss Lucy runs off.

The students are still.

Hannah She's losing her bloody marbles.

Laura It certainly seems that way.

Alfie Why's she acting like we don't know all of that already?

Ruth I think Hannah's right.

She's going a bit bonkers if you ask me.

One by one the students run off.

Until Kathy, Ruth and Tommy are left.

Tommy looks at Kathy.

Kathy looks at Tommy.

Ruth looks at Kathy.

Kathy Now I can see what Miss Lucy was worried about.

Tommy and Ruth disappear.

We all knew. But we didn't *understand*.

Phillip   But if they told you everything. Why wouldn't you understand?

Kathy   I think it's because of the way they told us. It was never straightforward. It was always mixed in with some other kind of information –

Miss Emily Missionary.

Miss Emily points to a slide projection that appears behind her while teaching the students. The image is a stick figure drawing of a man and woman lying on top of each other. The stick-figure penis can be seen penetrating the vagina internally.

The most common of the sexual positions.

Male on top. Female below. As you see the penis enters the vagina. Here.

Another slide appears.

Female on top of male.

This position provides the female with further stimulation of the clitoris which can be beneficial for reaching climax.

Another slide.

From behind.

The male is positioned behind the female and penetration occurs. Here.

Any questions?

Miss Emily looks to the students who are stunned into silence. Miss Emily then takes off her glasses. Looks at the students. Her tone less formal –

You must be careful *who* you have sex with.

Not just because of diseases. But because sex affects. Emotions. In ways you'd never expect.

In the outside world.

Sex has a different meaning.

People even fight and kill each other over who has sex with whom. And the reason it means so much more than say. Dancing or table-tennis. Is because the people out there.

The people out there.

Are different from you students.

They can have babies from sex.

That's why it's so important to them.

And even though it's completely impossible for any of you to have babies.

You have to respect the rules. And treat sex as.

Well as something rather special.

Miss Emily looks at the class. Then suddenly the slide changes.

Fellatio. The oral stimulation of –

Phillip Miss Emily made a load of sense if you ask me.

SCENE SIX: A WARD

Philip sits up in a hospital bed wearing a hospital gown. Kathy standing opposite.

Kathy   But it wasn't straightforward sense. Nothing she told us felt. Clear.

Phillip   And did you respect the rules? Did you treat sex as something. Special?

Kathy   I mean. As much as teenagers do.

Do you want anything?

Phillip   I wish I could have a drink. I'm parched.

Kathy   I know I'm sorry.

I got that squash you like. As soon as you're out I'll having it waiting for you.

Phillip looks at his hands.

Phillip   What about you?

Who were you doing it with?

Kathy   Do you remember back when we said one question?

Phillip laughs.

Phillip   Come on. I'm about to go in for a life-threatening operation.

Kathy   (*Tutting.*) Don't be ridiculous.

If you must know. I was something of a. Late developer.

Although I wasn't really aware of it at the time.

Ruth   Kath.

Kathy	Everyone was talking about doing it. But I assumed it was mostly bluster.
Ruth	Kathy can I ask you something?
Kathy	So I thought everyone else was the same as me.
	Inexperienced.

Kathy and Ruth (sixteen) are brushing their teeth next to one another before bed. They look at each other straight ahead, as if seeing one another in the sink mirrors in front of them.

Ruth	You get on with Tommy don't you?
Kathy	I suppose.
Ruth	Would you say you were friends?
	Like good friends?
Kathy	I don't know.
Ruth	Well would you ever want to. You know. Be more than friends?
Kathy	What on earth are you talking about?
Ruth	Well would you feel weird if something happened.
	Between me and Tommy.
Kathy	What? Like sex?
Ruth	(*Laughing.*) Oh Kath. You're such a prude.
	Yes. Like *sex*.
	It's just. I'm fairly certain he wants to do it with me.
	And I think he's okay. At least. He's better than most the boys in our year.
	But I wanted to check you hadn't got there first.

Kathy	No. No I would have told you if I'd.
	No.
Ruth	Okay.
	That's good.
	Because we already did it.
	Kathy drops her toothbrush.
	Don't say a word to Tommy.
	We said we wouldn't tell anyone.
	But I couldn't keep it from you Kath.
	Ruth brushes her teeth.
	Kathy looks dead ahead.
Kathy	What was it like?
Ruth	Yeah. I mean. Good I suppose.
	Actually. If I'm being honest.
	We've done it a few times.
Kathy	Oh.
	Okay.
	So are you like.
	A couple or something?
Ruth	No. I mean.
	Not really. I don't think.
	Maybe.
	I'm pretty sure he likes me.
	At least. He says he does.
	And I think I like him too Kath.

>   I really think I do.
>
>   *Ruth exits. Leaving Kathy.*
>
>   *Kathy looks dead ahead.*
>
>   *Still.*
>
>   *Stunned.*
>
>   *Her hand touches her heart.*
>
>   *Touches her heart.*

Admin   You're not surprised are you?

SCENE SEVEN: AN OFFICE

Kathy is opposite an Administrator sitting behind a desk.

Kathy   No. No it's just –

Admin   You look a little. Shocked –

Kathy   I'm not shocked. I just thought –

Admin   You did get a letter? You should have got a letter –

Kathy   Yes I got the letter. But I thought there was longer. That I had longer. It said three months and –

Admin   From when it was sent. Three months from when it was *sent*.

Kathy   I see.

Admin   Perhaps it got lost in the post.

Kathy   Yes.

Admin   But you've still got plenty of time.

(*Looking at a piece of paper.*) Four weeks.

Kathy	Yes.
Admin	Plenty of time to get everything in order.
Kathy	Yes.

Yes I've got plenty of.

Do you know where I'll be going? |
Admin	I'm sorry?
Kathy	Which centre I'll be going to?
Admin	Oh I'm not really supposed to –
Kathy	It's not Portsmouth is it?

It's just so cold there. In that centre and.

I'd really prefer it to be somewhere else.

The Administrator looks at the sheet of paper. |
| **Admin** | No.

It's not Portsmouth.

You should be pleased. With your work. It's been good. |
Kathy	Thank you.
Admin	It's very rare for someone to be a carer this long you know?
Kathy	Yes.
Admin	It's been what. Eleven years?
Kathy	Twelve. By the time I finish it'll.

Twelve. |
| **Admin** | And I'm sure they'd like you to carry on but. You're at an age now where things really have to start moving along and. |

	But everyone's pleased with your work. You should know that.
Kathy	I enjoy it.
	Being a carer.
	I've enjoyed it.
	Kathy turns to go.
Admin	You can always tell the ones from Hailsham.
	At the word 'Hailsham', there's a low, almost imperceptible hum.
	Tommy appears standing behind the Administrator.
	They're so much more.
	Substantial.
Tommy	You alright there Kath?
Kathy	Just thinking Tommy.
	The Administrator disappears.
Tommy	Looks like you're thinking really hard.
	Tommy pulls a face to imitate Kathy's 'serious thinking'.
	Come on then. What you thinking about this time?
Kathy	About how we'll be leaving here soon.
Tommy	I know. Mad isn't it.
	Hopefully they'll put us together after here.
	I can't imagine being anywhere without you there too.
	Kathy smiles.

You know what I was thinking about the other day?

Those Walkmans that have been at the last few Sales.

I know most of them are broken and stuff. But imagine if you'd had one that worked. Back when you had that tape Kath.

That tape you were obsessed with.

Kathy   *Songs After Dark?*

Tommy   Yeah! I was thinking. Imagine if Kathy had a Walkman back then.

She could have listened to that tape all day and night.

I reckon that would have made you really happy.

Kathy   I had no idea you even knew about that tape.

Tommy   Of course I did! You used to sneak off and listen to it all the time.

And I remember when you lost it.

Going around asking everyone if they'd seen it.

I hunted for days. Searched all the dorms and everything.

I wanted to be the one to find it for you.

Did you ever find out where it went?

Kathy shakes her head.

Kathy   It's gone to Norfolk.

Tommy   (*Laughing.*) That's right. It's gone to Norfolk.

Kathy You know. Something really weird happened with that tape once. Years ago.

Something I've never told anyone.

There was this one song on the album that I loved.

The song begins to play.

I used to play it in my dorm when no one else was there. And I created this story that went with it.

Tommy Did you imagine you were being swept off your feet?

Kathy No I was too young for anything like that! I was only about ten.

I imagined the song was about this woman who'd really wanted a baby. But she'd been told she couldn't have them. And there had been a sort of. Miracle. And so she had this baby after all.

Kathy picks up a pillow. Cradles it like a baby.

And she would sing to it. Partly because she was so happy. But also because she was really scared that something would happen to it.

That it would get ill or be taken away or something.

Kathy closes her eyes. Swaying to the music.

And this one time I was in my dorm listening to the song. Playing this story out in my head.

Kathy closes her eyes and sings along with Judy.

(*Singing.*)
Oh baby, baby.
Never let me –

Kathy stops. Opens her eyes.

(*Spoken.*) When I could suddenly feel. Someone was watching.

Kathy spins around.

And there. Standing in the doorway.

Was Madame.

Madame can now be seen. Peering through the partially open door. Staring at Kathy.

She was standing in the corridor. Totally still.

Watching me.

And crying.

Tommy *Crying?*

Kathy More than crying.

Sobbing.

And I stood there. Waiting for her to say something.

I mean she was the grown-up. She should have done something.

But she just stayed there. Rooted to the spot. Staring at me.

Sobbing.

Don't you think that's odd?

Madame disappears.

Tommy When she saw you dancing like that. Holding your pretend baby. She probably thought that was really tragic. How we can't have babies. And that's why she started crying.

Kathy	But how could she have known the song was anything to do with babies? That was just a made-up story in my head.
Tommy	Maybe Madame can read minds.
	They laugh.
	Maybe she can see inside you.
	Inside all of us.
	Kathy and Tommy stop laughing.
Ruth	There you are!
	Ruth runs up to them. Breathless.
Kathy	Hi Ruth.
Ruth	Have you heard the news?
	Miss Lucy's gone.
Tommy	Gone?
Kathy	What do you mean?
Ruth	Miss Emily was taking her classes this morning and announced that Miss Lucy is gone and isn't coming back.
	Tommy looks at Kathy.
Tommy	I wonder why.
Ruth	It's hardly a surprise. She's been acting loopy for ages now.
	Ruth approaches Tommy and kisses him on the lips.
	Brushes his hair out of his eyes.
	Oh you're all sweaty.
Tommy	I was playing football.

Ruth Ugh.

Tommy and Kathy avoid each other's eyes.

(*To Kathy.*) Have you had lunch?

Kathy Not yet.

Ruth Let's go then.

Ruth takes Tommy by the hand and starts to walk away with him.

Kathy remains.

Kathy!

Let's go!

Nurse 2 X-rays and blood tests are due tomorrow.

SCENE EIGHT: THE ROOM

A Nurse is reading from a chart. The sounds of hospital machinery can be heard. Phillip is lying in the bed. Eyes closed.

Kathy And how is he?

Nurse 2 I mean his vitals look alright. But.

The Nurse makes a gesture to say 'not good'.

Kathy Was he asking for anything in particular?

Nurse 2 Just you. I think he wants to chat. Says he likes your stories.

(*Calling to the bed.*) You said you liked her stories didn't you?

A groan from the bed.

Call me if anything happens.

The Nurse exits.

Kathy looks at Phillip.

Phillip Is she gone?

Kathy Yes.

Phillip tries to sit up. Vocalised pain.

Don't get up. It's okay.

Phillip I can't stand her.

Kathy smiles.

Kathy How you feeling?

Phillip Can I have some water?

Kathy pours water from a jug into a cup. Helps Phillip as he sips from it.

Was she telling you it hadn't gone well?

Kathy No. She said everything was fine.

Phillip It wasn't fine.

I'm not fine.

Kathy This is always the hardest part.

Phillip It's only my first. It should be easier than this.

Kathy It's different for everyone.

You'll be feeling better soon.

Phillip closes his eyes with the pain.

Do you want me to call her?

He gives a small shake of the head.

What do you need?

Phillip Talk to me.

Tell me something.

Kathy	Well.
	The rain hasn't stopped.
Phillip	Not the fucking weather.
	Kathy looks away. Considers.
Kathy	It finally happened.
	I got my notice.
Phillip	So I'm your last?
Kathy	One of my last. I do have other donors you know.
Phillip	Yeah. But I'm the best of the last.
	Kathy laughs.
Kathy	It would be very unprofessional of me to say.
	But I've enjoyed our time.
Phillip	Maybe they'll place you here.
	And we can be donors together.
	Kathy smiles.
Kathy	Maybe.
Phillip	Thank you.
Kathy	What for?
Phillip	For giving me.
	He struggles to speak.
	Your memories.
	Kathy looks at Phillip. Smiles.
	Phillip indicates he wants more water. Kathy helps him drink.
	He settles back. Looks at Kathy.

	What happened with Ruth and Tommy?
Kathy	They broke up just before our final term.
Phillip	Who broke up with who?
Kathy	I honestly can't remember. I think Ruth had a thing with Alfie. And then Tommy had a thing with Martha. And then it all sort of. Dissolved.
Phillip	Did you seize your moment?

Kathy looks at Phillip.

Shakes her head.

Did you at least tell him. How you felt about him?

Kathy   I'm not sure I knew myself.

I mean I knew I felt something for him.

But I didn't understand what that feeling was.

And then. A few weeks before we left.

I decided to act.

Tommy appears, kicking a football by himself.

In a way that I thought was right.

Tommy looks over and sees Kathy beckoning him over. He goes to her.

Tommy I have to tell you something.

The thing is.

She looks away.

The thing is.

We're leaving Hailsham really soon and. And who knows where we'll end up.

But I think it's really important.

	Really important.
	That before we go.
	I tell you something.
Tommy	It's alright Kath.
	You can say it.
	Kathy looks at Tommy.
	Tommy looks at Kathy.
Kathy	You have to get back with Ruth.
Tommy	What?! **Phillip** What?!
Kathy	She wants to get back together. And it's the best thing for both of you.
Tommy	Kath. Why are you getting involved in this?
Kathy	Because Ruth asked me to ask you and.
	I think it's a good chance for you.
	She cares about you Tommy.
	She cares about you very much.
Tommy	I don't know.
	I don't know if that's right.
	I don't know.
Kathy	Do you have any idea how lucky you are?
	Of all the people you've got Ruth fancying you.
	And they keep couples together a lot of the time.
	So if you're with Ruth when we leave. That's the best outcome you could hope for Tommy.
Tommy	Is that what you think Kath?

>   That's what you really think?
>
>   That I should be with Ruth?
>
>   *Tommy looks at Kathy.*
>
>   *Kathy looks at Tommy.*

Phillip   Why?

Kathy   I don't know.

              It felt easier.

              And sometimes we convince ourselves that the easy thing. Is the right thing.

              Even if it isn't.

              Anyway we left Hailsham shortly after that.

Phillip   Were you sad to leave?

Kathy   Not sad exactly.

              We were excited at the prospect of growing up. Seeing new things.

              But by the time we actually left I think I was more. Shocked.

              We all were.

              We had no idea that Hailsham was so different to everywhere else. That *we'd* be so different.

              I think that's why Hailsham closed down in the end.

              Because it was so different.

Phillip   Where did they send you?

Kathy   Some went to the White Mansion in the Welsh hills.

              Others to Poplar Farm in Dorset.

The sound of thunder and rain.

Ruth. Tommy. Laura and myself.

We were sent to the Cottages.

Kathy lifts the hood of her coat as Ruth, Tommy and Hannah appear next to her, all wearing overcoats with hoods.

Chrissie   Hi. Hi!

Hello.

A projection appears: 'PART TWO: THE COTTAGES'.

Chrissie appears calling out to them.

You must be the newbies.

She's holding a newspaper over her head to protect her from the rain.

Don't you want to come in?

The Hailsham crew look at one another.

Ruth   Yes. Yes we do.

Ruth follows Chrissie, the others joining as they enter –

SCENE NINE: A KITCHEN

Chrissie   I'm Chrissie.

This is Rodney.

Rodney   Hi.

Ruth, Kathy, Tommy and Laura stand huddled together in their coats. Rodney leans against the counter. Eating toast and drinking tea.

Chrissie	The others are around somewhere. Come in come in.
	We were laughing at you. Weren't we Rod?
Rodney	We were.
Chrissie	Watching you all standing there like terrified little rabbits.
	Rodney does an impression of their terrified expressions. Chrissie laughs, putting her arm around Rodney. Rodney reciprocates.
	I said I have to go and get them before they die of cold.
Ruth	We weren't sure where to go.
Rodney	It can feel like a bit of a maze this place.
Tommy	There was a man who saw us. But he didn't say anything.
Chrissie	That's Keffers.
Rodney	Miserable old bastard.
Chrissie	He works here. Comes around about three days a week.
Rodney	He's supposed to fix the stuff that's broken.
Chrissie	Not that he ever does.
Rodney	Or if he does he'll bloody well moan about it.
Chrissie	Oh God look at you all standing there. Take your coats off.
Rodney	Do you want a cuppa?
Chrissie	Or some toast?
Kathy	Is this where we'll be living?

Chrissie	Some of you will be in here.
Rodney	This is the farmhouse.
Chrissie	There's the outhouses too. Lots of people are in them. They're all pretty good. Though it can get a bit cold in the winter.
Rodney	A bit? It's fucking freezing.
Chrissie	But we've got loads of blankets and heaters and things.
Rodney	If Keffers ever brings them.
	Lenny enters.
Lenny	Is this the new lot?
Chrissie	They've just arrived.
	I've suddenly realised I don't know your names!
Ruth	I'm Ruth. That's Laura. Tommy and Kathy.
Lenny	Lenny.
Chrissie	We were just telling them about Keffers.
Lenny	Miserable old fucker.
	Chrissie and Rodney laugh.
Chrissie	See?
Lenny	(*Indicating Tommy and Kathy.*) Are you a couple?
Chrissie	Oh. Lenny's on the lookout already.
	Chrissie and Rodney laugh.
Lenny	Piss off.
Ruth	No we're a couple.
	Ruth puts her arm around Tommy.

Kathy looks away.

But Kathy and Laura are free agents.

Laura   Thank you Ruth.

Kathy   How long have you been here?

Rodney   We're starting our second year.

Chrissie   Can't believe it. It's gone so fast.

Lenny   We just said goodbye to the veterans this week.

Rodney   That's what we call the people who were here before us.

Lenny   I suppose we're the veterans now.

Chrissie   Oh yeah! I suppose we are.

Lenny   So where are you all from?

Rodney   Are you from the same place?

Chrissie   Rodney and I were at Riders. Near Maidstone.

Tommy   That sounds nice.

Rodney   I'm not sure *nice* is the word I'd use.

Lenny   Yeah Palmers wasn't very *nice* either.

Chrissie Rodney and Lenny laugh.

A little too hard.

Bloody glad that's done with.

Chrissie   This is so much better. Isn't it Rod?

Rodney   So much.

Kathy   We're from Hailsham.

Chrissie, Rodney and Lenny stop.

They stop.

Chrissie	*Hailsham?*
Lenny	Bloody hell.
Tommy	Do you know it?
Rodney	We know *of* it.
	Chrissie, Rodney and Lenny look at the others.
	Look.
Chrissie	Hailsham. Wow.
	Chrissie looks at Tommy and Ruth.
	Are you applying for a deferral?
Tommy	What's a deferral?
Lenny	You must know if you're from there.
Ruth	Of course we know.
Tommy	We do?
Ruth	Don't be stupid Tommy.
	So what's the routine here? Who do we report to?
Rodney	No one really.
Chrissie	There's a rota of chores and things that we need to keep up with.
Rodney	Odd jobs around the place.
Lenny	Maintenance. Cleaning. That kind of thing.
	Keffers gets on at you if you're not keeping up with it.
Chrissie	And then there's your appointments and check-ups.
	But there's a good amount of free time too.

Laura	Can I take my stuff to my room?
Lenny	Sure. I'll show you round. Introduce you to the others.
Rodney	David and Sarah and that lot are in the barn I think.
	They take their coats and Lenny leads them to the door.
	I just can't believe you're from Hailsham.
Chrissie	I know.
	Hailsham.
	Isn't that mad?
	Laugh track.
Wife	(*Voice-over, American.*) Now what did I tell you about that sweetie?

SCENE TEN: A LIVING ROOM

Rodney, Chrissie, Ruth, Lenny and Laura are sitting on the sofa and the floor watching TV. Kathy sits with them, reading a book. From the TV American sitcom dialogue emanates. Every time the laugh track plays, everyone laughs. Except Kathy.

Wife I'm only saying –

Husband (*Voice-over, American.*) You're busting my balls is what you're doing.

Laugh track.

Chrissie I love the way she pulls that face behind his back!

Ruth So funny!

Tommy enters.

Tommy   What you watching?

Ruth   Shhh.

Husband   I told you I like to do it my way.

Wife   Oh okay. So it's *your* way that's to blame for THIS?!

Laugh track.

Tommy   Have I seen this one?

Ruth   Quiet Tommy.

Chrissie, Rodney, Lenny, Laura and Ruth all say the husband's last line with him:

Husband   Now sweetie. That is NOT what it looks like!

Laugh track and applause.

Rodney   It's brilliant the way he gets so worked up.

Chrissie ejects the VHS tape from the machine. Puts it back in its case.

Tommy   Is that one of the ones I've seen?

Ruth   I don't know Tommy. I can't keep track of everything you've watched.

Laura   We should see if we can barbecue food in the summer.

Rodney   Yes! That's a great idea.

Chrissie   I doubt Keffers would allow it sweetie.

Rodney   You're such a *spoilsport* sweetie.

Rodney puts his arm around Chrissie. They kiss on the lips.

Lenny nudges Laura. Gives a small wink. Laura nods. They stand.

Lenny   Night everyone.

Laura   See you tomorrow.

'Night' from the others as Lenny and Laura exit.

Ruth puts her arm around Tommy. Kisses him on the lips.

Ruth   Come on then sweetie.

Tommy   I was going to watch something.

Ruth   It's not the time to watch something sweetie. Everyone's going to bed.

Rodney   Ruth.

There's something we wanted to tell you.

Chrissie   It's not bad or anything.

You remember last week when Rodney and I went for some checks? Well we were at this centre on the Norfolk coast.

And while I was in there. Rodney went off to look around the town.

Rodney   I was wandering down these side streets off the main road –

Chrissie   And he passed this office –

Rodney   This big office with a massive glass window at the front –

Chrissie   And he was looking inside when he saw something –

Rodney   I couldn't believe it –

Chrissie   He swore on his life when he told me –

Rodney   I'd bet money on it.

	She was definitely.
	Is definitely.
Chrissie	Your original.
Tommy	Her what?
Rodney	Your possible.
	Isn't that what you call them?
	'*Possibles.*'
	Ruth, Kathy and Tommy look at Rodney.
Kathy	Are you serious?
Chrissie	Totally.
Tommy	What did she look like?
Rodney	Like Ruth!
Chrissie	*Exactly* like Ruth Rodney said.
Rodney	But older obviously.
Chrissie	And get this. She was working in an *office*.
	Isn't that mad Ruth?
Tommy	Why is that mad?
Chrissie	Because Ruth's going to work in an office.
	After here.
	Kathy and Tommy look at Ruth.
Rodney	That's got to be more than a coincidence.
Tommy	How are you going to work in an office?
Ruth	Will you shut up Tommy and leave me to think?
	You really reckon it was her?

Rodney	Absolutely. She was sitting at this desk drinking tea. Then she stood up and started talking to a man.
Ruth	What man?
Rodney	Just a man.
Ruth	What was she wearing?
Rodney	I can't remember. A jacket and a shirt? With trousers maybe.
Chrissie	We thought we could take you. So you could go and see for yourself.
Rodney	Yeah we could drive you up there to see.
Chrissie	We could all go up.

Make a day of it.

What do you think?

Kathy looks at Ruth.

Ruth looks at Kathy.

They burst out laughing. |

SCENE ELEVEN: A BEDROOM

Kathy and Ruth are sitting on Kathy's bed. Drinking tea.

Ruth	And you didn't tell him to stop doing it?
Kathy	How could I?

Besides I don't think he knows he *is* doing it.

Kathy imitates David's sex noises.

They laugh.

So hard the laughter is silent. |

So hard their stomachs ache.

No we shouldn't. We shouldn't.

David's nice. Underneath.

Ruth Underneath all the noises.

They laugh.

The laughter dies.

Kathy I think Miss Emily was right though.

After having these one-nighters. The sex does do funny things to my feelings.

Ruth Maybe ease off them for a while.

Wait until you find someone you want to be in a couple with.

Kathy drinks her tea.

Ruth drinks her tea.

Kathy Do you ever get so you just really have to do it?

Like a kind of. Urge to do it. With anybody almost.

Ruth I'm in a couple so if I want to do it I just do it with Tommy.

Kathy No but. Do you ever feel like you just *need* to do it?

Like when David started snogging me. At first I wanted him to get off.

But then this feeling just came on out of nowhere.

And it was like I suddenly. Had to do it.

Ruth That sounds a bit strange Kath.

Kathy	Maybe there's something. Not quite right with me.
Ruth	It's probably the different food we're eating here.

They drink their tea.

It's a shame though. I thought you and David could be a good couple.

Kathy	I don't mind.
Ruth	But it's a shame you haven't found someone you really like.

Like I found Tommy.

They drink their tea.

Drink.

Can you believe this stuff about my possible?

Kathy	Do you really think it's her?
Ruth	Rodney seems pretty certain.

Imagine if I actually get to meet her.

What would I say?

Kathy	Start by saying hello I suppose.
Ruth	What just bowl up. 'Hello my name is Ruth C. And I was cloned from you.'

She'd run a mile.

Kathy	Well she'll probably know who you are from looking at you.

You'd be identical after all.

Ruth	(*Laughing.*) Yeah.
Kathy	Do you think our possibles volunteered?

Or do you think they got paid?

Ruth   I think you're thinking too much about stuff that doesn't matter as usual.

Ruth drinks her tea.

Kathy   Chrissie and Rodney keep bringing up this deferral business.

Ruth   It's just a rumour that the non-Hailsham lot talk about.

Kathy   What does it mean?

Ruth   I've no idea.

Kathy   But you told them you knew what they were.

Ruth   I was just getting them off our backs.

Kathy looks at her tea.

Looks at her tea.

Kathy   Ruth.

            Why do you call Tommy 'sweetie'?

Ruth   What?

Kathy   You've started calling him that. Ever since you got here.

Ruth   So what? It's no big deal. A lot of us do it.

Kathy   You mean Chrissie and Rodney do it.

Ruth   Oh so *that's* your problem.

Kathy   I'm just saying it's daft. The way you copy everything Chrissie and Rodney do.

Ruth   Ruth's got new friends and baby sister's all upset –

Kathy   *Tommy sweetie. Can you pass the salt sweetie. Thank you sweetie.* It's not how normals talk.

Ruth You're all upset because I've managed to move on and make new friends and most of the veterans don't even know your name –

Kathy I've made friends –

Ruth Hardly. You won't talk to anyone unless they're Hailsham.

Kathy Well at least I don't treat Tommy like dirt all the time. You're constantly leaving him in the lurch like a spare part. You're supposed to be a couple Ruth. That means you should be looking out for him.

Ruth That's right Kathy. We're a couple. And what we do is none of your business.

But if you must know. Tommy and I have talked about it. And if he doesn't want to do things with Chrissie and Rodney then he's agreed that he shouldn't hold me back.

Because that's what couples do Kathy. They talk stuff through. But you wouldn't know that because you've never been with anyone.

At least. Not for more than one night.

Kathy looks at Ruth.

Looks at Ruth.

Nurse 3 I'm afraid not.

SCENE TWELVE: A RECEPTION AREA

A Nurse sits behind a desk. Kathy talking to her.

Kathy But no one called me.

Nurse 3 Didn't they?

That's odd.

What's your name?

Kathy Kathy. Kathy H.

The Nurse looks at her notes.

Nurse 3 Ah. It says here you're no longer his carer.

Kathy But I've got another week before I –

Nurse 3 That's why they didn't call.

(*Off the notes.*) Unusual.

Completing after a first donation.

He can't have been very strong.

Kathy No he was strong. He was very.

I think it might have been more about the donation.

Nurse 3 Alright.

We'll have none of that.

Kathy Sorry.

Nurse 3 That's not the kind of talk we have around here.

Kathy Yes I. Sorry.

Did he leave anything?

Nurse 3 Like what?

Kathy I don't know. A message or a.

	Can I go to his room?
	I bought him some things that he might have left.
Nurse 3	The room's been taken by someone else.
	Let me see if anything's here.
	The Nurse looks behind the desk.
	All I have is an old quiz book.
	Spot the difference.
	Kathy takes the puzzle book.
	Looks at it.
	Did you know him long?
Kathy	What? Oh. No not really.
	But he was.
	He helped me.
	She holds the book to her chest.
Nurse 3	Do what?
	Tommy appears. He looks at Kathy.
Kathy	Look at things.
	Things I was afraid of.
	Ruth appears. She looks at Kathy.
	Things I needed to see.
	Laughter.
Rodney	He is absolutely hysterical.

SCENE THIRTEEN: A CAFÉ

Chrissie, Rodney, Ruth, Kathy and Tommy are sat at a table, eating sandwiches.

Chrissie and Rodney are laughing uncontrollably. Ruth joins them.

Chrissie He could imitate your walk and voice and everything.

Chrissie and Rodney laugh. Ruth laughs with them.

You know he isn't far from here. We should go and see him.

Rodney Yes! That's a brilliant idea.

Kathy What's he doing?

Chrissie He's a carer.

Ruth Obviously.

Chrissie (*As if explaining to a child.*) That's what you do after you leave the Cottages Kathy. You become a carer.

Kathy Yes I know. What I mean is.

We can't just go and visit him can we?

We're not allowed.

Rodney (*Wagging his finger.*) Oh it would be naughty-naughty to visit Martin.

Ruth Kathy *hates* being naughty. Don't you Kath?

Tommy Whereabouts is this office then?

The one with Ruth's possible.

Rodney It was a turning off the High Street. Down the other end.

	It's an office with big windows.
	Ruth tries to suppress a smile.
Chrissie	Before we go.
	We wanted to talk to you.
	About the deferrals.
Tommy	I still don't know what this deferrals stuff means.
Ruth	Tommy's a bit slow about things. Aren't you Tommy.
Tommy	Well do you know what it means?
Rodney	A deferral's where you get your donations delayed.
Chrissie	It's really rare for them to do it. But they say Hailsham will give you a deferral if you're in a couple and can show to them.
	Prove to them.
	That you're properly.
	Truly.
	In love.
Rodney	If you can prove that. The people at Hailsham sort it out for you so you can have a few years together.
Kathy	A few *years*?
Chrissie	Three or four apparently.
Rodney	Before you begin your donations.
Chrissie	But what we want to know is.
	Is it only Hailsham students who can apply?
Rodney	Or is there some way we could.

	Some way other people could.
Chrissie	Try.

Chrissie and Rodney look to Ruth.

Ruth opens her mouth to respond, but no words come. Kathy jumps in –

Kathy	They never told us anything like that. They want to keep it quiet I'm guessing or they'd be overrun.
Ruth	Yes it's not the sort of thing they'd advertise.
Chrissie	Do you think you could look into it?
Ruth	We can try.
Rodney	Imagine.
	Three or four *years*.

Kathy looks at Tommy.

Ruth looks at Tommy.

Tommy looks out.

| **Tommy** | So which one is it? |

SCENE FOURTEEN: NORFOLK

Chrissie, Rodney, Ruth, Tommy and Kathy stand in a line looking out. Their hands cupped as they peer into an unseen office.

Tommy	Which one's Ruth's possible?
	They peer in.
	Peer in.
	Peer.
Rodney	There! Over there in that corner.

>
> She's talking to that big red woman.
>
> *Their eyes fixed in unison on the Possible.*
>
> *Their eyes follow her together, across the unseen space.*

Tommy   Bloody hell.

Rodney   It's amazing isn't it?

Chrissie   Her hair and eyes and everything.

Kathy   Even the way she moves.

> *Someone in the office has spotted them, and they all instantly turn away from the window.*
>
> *They huddle together. Laugh nervously. Except Ruth.*
>
> *Ruth stands slightly apart from them. Silent. Still.*

Tommy   I can't believe it.

Rodney   You can see why I had to say something –

Chrissie   Even her smile's the same –

Kathy   Ruth?

Tommy   She looks really smart –

Chrissie   *Really* smart –

Rodney   It's got to be her. It's got to be.

Kathy   Ruth?

> What do you think?
>
> *They all look to Ruth.*
>
> *Ruth looks towards the office.*
>
> *Looks.*

Ruth	It's a real office.
	And she's a real office lady.
Rodney	You should go and talk to her.
Ruth	I can't.
Chrissie	You have to! She's your possible!
Tommy	Look! There she is. Look!
	The Possible exits the office. She's in corporate attire. Her hair colour and stature the same as Ruth's.
	She walks across the space, looking for something in her handbag.
	They watch her.
	Then, just before she's gone –
	Excuse me!
	The Possible turns and faces them.
	They stare at her.
	Stare.
Possible	Yes?
	Stare.
	What do you want?
Tommy	Nothing.
	It's.
	Nothing.
	The Possible looks at Tommy and the others. Shakes her head.
Possible	You lot shouldn't be bothering people.

The Possible turns and exits.

Ruth Why the hell did you do that Tommy?

Tommy Well I thought you wanted to meet her.

See her properly. Up close.

Ruth That was such a stupid thing to do.

I can't believe you'd do something so stupid.

Kathy I think Tommy just wanted to help you see her better.

Ruth Yes I'm aware of that Kathy thank you.

Ruth turns her back to the others. Her hands balling and releasing fists.

Chrissie Alright so.

Seeing her up close like that.

I think it's safe to say.

She isn't Ruth's possible after all.

But you can see why Rodney thought she was.

Rodney She looked identical in there.

Tommy It doesn't matter anyway. It was just a bit of fun.

Kathy No it doesn't matter.

Tommy All this stuff about possibles is just a bit of fun.

Isn't it Ruth?

Ruth continues looking out.

And even if she had been your possible.

It wouldn't have made any difference to anything.

Ruth looks out.

Silent tears falling.

Kathy   Tommy's right. Who our possibles are doesn't change anything.

Tommy   Yeah. It was just a bit of fun.

Ruth   Tommy will you shut up with this 'bit of fun' stuff. It's pathetic.

Rodney   How about we go and see Martin? His flat's pretty close to here.

Chrissie   Yes! Martin's so funny. He'll have us in stitches in no time.

Ruth   I knew it was stupid. I knew it right from the start.

I didn't want to say anything when you first told me about it. But I knew it was never going to be her.

They don't use people like that.

We all know it.

We're not modelled from that sort –

Kathy   Ruth –

Ruth   Well we all know it Kathy. We all know it so let's just be honest.

We're modelled from *trash*. Junkies. Prostitutes. Winos. Convicts. We're modelled from the dregs. From shit. Just as long as they're not psychos.

That's what we come from.

We all know it so why don't we say it?

A bit of fun Tommy? A bit of fun? Let's all pretend I was modelled off a woman like that. WHAT FUN!

If you want to look for your possible. Do it properly. And look in the gutter.

Look in rubbish bins.

Look down the toilet.

That's where we've all come from.

Doctor And your last assessment was in October?

SCENE FIFTEEN: A DOCTOR'S OFFICE

Kathy sits opposite Female Doctor.

Kathy Yes.

The Doctor shines light into Kathy's eye. Then the other.

Makes a note. Reads something.

Doctor You're older than average for your first.

Kathy I've been a carer for a long time.

Doctor Yes. Yes I see that.

Alright well everything's in order so I think we're good to.

Oh wait. How stupid of me.

The Doctor grabs a blood-pressure monitor.

I forgot to do this.

She wraps it around Kathy's arm. Inflates the arm monitor.

Waits for the reading.

Do you know which centre you're going to?

Kathy Not yet.

They usually don't tell you until right before you –

Doctor Shit. It hasn't.

Sorry. I have to do it again.

The Doctor undoes the monitor and inflates it again.

Kathy You're new aren't you?

Doctor Is it that obvious?

Kathy I wasn't implying you were bad or anything.

You're just more.

You're nicer than the others.

Doctor (*Reading the monitor.*) Finally!

She makes a note of the reading. Removes the arm monitor.

You must have been a good carer. To have done it so long.

Kathy I just did the obvious things really.

Doctor What are they?

Kathy If they want to talk. Listen.

And if they want to listen. Talk.

And if they don't want to talk or listen. You're just.

There.

	It's about having another person with you. Because.

It's about having another person with you. Because.

It's scary.

Even for us.

The Doctor suddenly drops the blood-pressure monitor. She stands. Flustered.

Doctor You can go now.

Kathy picks up her jacket. Puts it on.

Come on now. I've got to get on.

Kathy turns back to the Doctor.

Looks at her.

Looks.

Kathy I don't want to go.

SCENE SIXTEEN: NORFOLK

Rodney Come on Kath. Don't be like that.

Chrissie Rodney Ruth and Tommy are standing on the cliffs. They look at Kathy.

Chrissie You'll like Martin. He's a real laugh.

You're coming aren't you Ruth?

Kathy Ruth can go. But I'm not.

Ruth Kathy's all upset because I said the truth about our possibles.

Kathy It's nothing to do with that.

I don't want to visit a carer. We're not supposed to and I don't even know this Martin person.

Ruth Let her go off on her own and sulk if she wants to. I don't care.

Rodney Okay well.

Meet us by the car at four.

Rodney, Chrissie and Ruth start to go.

Tommy I think I'll stay here with Kath.

Ruth Fine.

Do whatever you want Tommy.

Rodney, Chrissie and Ruth exit.

Kathy sits on the ground. Looking out.

Tommy joins her.

The sound of waves can be heard in the distance.

Tommy It's just what people say when they're feeling sorry for themselves.

Our possibles. What they were like.

It has nothing to do with us.

Kathy looks out.

Kathy But we all wonder about who our possible is. About who we're modelled off. That's why we all came out here today.

We wouldn't care so much if it didn't mean anything.

Tommy What difference does it make though really? It wouldn't change anything.

Kathy But it might explain some things about why we're the way we are.

	Sometimes I get these really strong feelings. Like urges. And.
	It just comes over me and I know it's weird. But then I do it with one of the guys and it never feels right and.
	What if I'm like that because my possible was some kind of. I don't know.
	Pervert or something.
Tommy	I think most people get those feelings at times Kath. In fact.
	If I'm honest.
	I feel like that quite a lot.
	He laughs. Looks at Kathy.
	Kathy starts to cry.
	Tommy puts his arm around her shoulders.
	Remember what Miss Emily used to say?
	When you do it with someone you really want to be with.
	Then it will be really good.
	It'll make you feel really good.
Kathy	Sorry. I don't know why I'm letting this stuff get to me so much.
	It's just so different here. And Ruth's being so.
	I don't know.
Tommy	I think she's struggling with being here too.
	More than she'd like to admit.
Kathy	Are you struggling?

Tommy shrugs.

Tommy I thought everywhere was the same as Hailsham.

Turns out Hailsham's different to everywhere else.

Kathy bumps shoulders with Tommy.

They look out.

Look.

What do you think about that deferral stuff? About people having their donations delayed if they're in love.

Kathy We've no idea if it's true or not.

Tommy But what if it is true?

Don't you think it could explain quite a lot of stuff we used to puzzle over?

Kathy Like what?

Tommy The Gallery for starters. We never got to the bottom of what the Gallery was for. Why Madame took away all our best work.

But you remember that time Miss Emily said it was very important? Because our artwork revealed what you were like *inside*.

She said it revealed *your soul*.

Kathy Yes.

Tommy Well what if some special arrangement *has* been made for Hailsham students? They'd need a way to know wouldn't they. Which couples were just a crush and which ones were really. Truly.

In love.

And Madame's got a gallery filled with stuff from when we were tiny.

So if two people go and say they're in love. She can find the art they've done over years and years.

And see what they're like.

Inside.

See if they really are a true match.

Kathy looks at Tommy.

Only thing is. I've blown my chance.

I mean I never really bothered with being creative did I?

Kathy It's only a theory Tommy.

Maybe they've got lots of ways to judge.

Maybe the art's just one of those ways.

Kathy looks at Tommy.

Tommy looks at Kathy.

They continue looking at one another as the sound of waves crashing gets louder.

Louder.

Louder.

Suddenly the light and sound shifts.

I can't believe you found it.

SCENE SEVENTEEN: A LIVING ROOM

Tommy It was that day in Norfolk. After the others went off.

We went into that charity shop. Remember?

And I thought. Wouldn't it be amazing. If after all these years. Kath's lost tape was in Norfolk after all.

So while you were looking at the books I had a rummage and. There it was.

Your Judy Bridgewater.

I was waiting for the right time to give it to you.

You've seemed a bit down lately so. I thought it might cheer you up.

Kathy looks at the tape. Smiles.

Kathy Thank you Tommy.

Thank you.

Kathy looks at Tommy.

Tommy Kath.

I've started doing some drawings.

He pulls out a small notebook. Hands it to Kathy.

They're animals. Imaginary animals that I've been thinking up.

Kathy looks at the pages in the notebook.

I'm doing them really small. Tiny. I'd never thought of that at Hailsham. I think maybe that's where I went wrong. If you make them tiny everything changes.

It's like they come to life by themselves. I worry about them as I'm creating them. About how they'd protect themselves. How they'd reach things.

Things like that.

Kathy continues looking through the pages. Tommy watching her.

I'll have to get a lot better before Madame sees them.

Kathy looks at Tommy.

Not that I'm doing them because of all that.

I like doing them.

What do you think?

Kathy	I think you should be really proud of these Tommy.
Tommy	You do?
Kathy	I really do.

Tommy tries to suppress a smile.

He takes the notebook back.

Holds out his little finger.

Kathy links her little finger with his.

Ruth Are you coming to say goodbye to Lenny?

Ruth pops her head round the door.

Kathy	Yes.	**Tommy**	Yes coming.
Ruth	What are you two up to?		
Kathy	Just chatting.	**Tommy**	Nothing.

Ruth looks at them.

Looks.

Ruth What's that?

Ruth points to Kathy's hand.

Kathy Oh this.

It's just a tape.

Ruth takes the tape. Looks at it.

Ruth It's the one you had at Hailsham.

Kathy Yes.

Ruth Where d'you get it?

Kathy Tommy found it.

Ruth Did you?

Where?

Tommy It was that day in Norfolk.

You'd gone off with Chrissie and Rodney to meet their friend remember?

Kathy and I were in a charity shop and I happened to come across it.

Ruth Wow.

How very. Considerate of you Tommy.

Quite the find.

Why didn't you tell me about it?

About finding Kathy's prized tape?

Tommy I forgot all about it until today. I saw it in my bag just now.

Kathy Turns out Norfolk is the lost corner after all.

Ruth nods. Half smiles.

Hands the tape back to Kathy.

Ruth Are you coming to say goodbye to Lenny or not?

Tommy walks to Ruth.

Ruth takes Tommy's hand.

Kathy watches them go.

She looks at the tape in her hand.

'Never Let Me Go' by Judy Bridgewater plays.

Kathy closes her eyes. Sways to the music.

Sways to the music.

Caught you.

Kathy spins round in shock.

SCENE EIGHTEEN: A BEDROOM

Kathy rushes to a Fisher-Price tape player and turns off the music.

Ruth's holding two mugs.

Ruth I got you a hot chocolate.

Kathy Oh. Thanks.

Ruth hands the hot chocolate to Kathy. Sits on Kathy's bed. Pats the space next to her.

Kathy sits.

Ruth I wanted to say sorry.

Kathy What for?

Ruth For being a bit of an arse these past few weeks.

Ruth looks at her mug.

	If I'm being honest. That stuff about my possible sort of threw me and.

I don't know Kath.

Sometimes I think I'm doing alright here. And then other times.

Anyway. I'm sorry.

Kathy I'm sorry too.

They look at one another and smile.

Laugh. Embarrassed by their emotion.

Ruth I saw you hanging around with Michael.

Kathy shakes her head.

No?

Kathy He's got this weird. Smell.

Ruth laughs.

Kathy laughs.

Ruth You're too bloody picky. That's your problem.

Kathy I can't help it!

Ruth laughs.

Kathy laughs.

Ruth I've missed this.

Kathy I've missed it too.

They drink their hot chocolate.

Ruth. Can I ask you something?

Did you tell Chrissie you were going to work in an office?

Ruth What? No!

	That's just Chrissie. Getting carried away as usual.
	She's got this thing about Hailsham people being able to do anything they want.
Kathy	So she didn't get that from you?
Ruth	Of course not. She just has these bonkers ideas.
	Like the way she keeps going on about the deferrals.
Kathy	Don't you think that's true?
Ruth	I mean it could be I suppose.
	I haven't really thought about it.
	Ruth drinks her hot chocolate.
	Has Tommy shown you his new art project?
Kathy	His drawings? Yeah.
Ruth	All those weird animals.
	I didn't know what to say when he showed me.
	There's one that's like an eagle and a horse mashed together.
	And it looks like it's wearing massive underpants.
	Ruth laughs.
	Kathy joins her.
	And there's that other one that looks like a squashed hedgehog with horns.
	Ruth laughs.
	Kathy joins her.
	He was always rubbish at art. So why he's suddenly doing it again I've no idea.

Kathy drinks her hot chocolate.

Ruth looks at her mug.

Looks at her mug.

Kath.

There's something I've been wanting to tell you.

I just never quite know how to say it. Or when really. And.

Promise you won't be cross with me? Because I have to tell you this Kath.

For your own good.

Kathy You can say it. I won't be cross.

Ruth I'm sure you can see that me and Tommy might not be a couple forever.

And now there's all this talk about couples getting deferrals if they can prove.

You know.

That they're really meant to be.

Together.

It would be completely natural if you'd thought about. What would happen if me and Tommy. If we decided we shouldn't be together any more.

But the thing is Kathy.

The thing is.

I know how he feels about you.

I know because he's told me.

And you need to know. You deserve to know.

That Tommy doesn't see you like that.

He really really likes you. He thinks you're great.

Really great.

But he would never want you to be a. Proper girlfriend or anything because.

God this is really hard to say.

Because.

Tommy doesn't like girls who've been. You know.

With lots of people.

He has a thing about it.

And he knows you've had all these one-nighters here.

And he'd never be able to get past that.

I'm sorry Kath. But I had to tell you for your own good.

I hope you understand.

Kathy looks at her mug.

Looks.

Kathy Thank you for telling me.

Ruth What you've got to understand though is that he thinks the world of you.

He really does.

We both do.

Kathy looks at Ruth.

Half smiles.

She suddenly jumps up. The light and sound shifting as she does. She spins around and –

Kathy There you are!

SCENE NINETEEN: A FIELD

Kathy walks towards Tommy and Ruth who are leaning against the barn.

Kathy I've been trying to find you all morning.

Kathy looks at Ruth and Tommy.

Have I interrupted something?

Ruth looks at Tommy.

Tommy looks at his feet.

Ruth Tommy's been telling me about his big theory.

His big gallery theory.

About how our artwork would be used as proof for deferrals.

But apparently he's already told you about this.

Apparently he told you. *Ages ago.*

Kathy It's not a bad theory. It might be right.

Ruth I had to really dig it out of Tommy boy here didn't I? Not very keen on letting me in on it at all. Were you sweetie?

It was only when I kept pressing him on what was behind all this *art*.

Tommy I'm not doing it just for that.

All I said was if the theory *was* right. I could try and submit my animals –

Ruth Tommy don't make a fool of yourself in front of our friend.

Tommy I don't see why it's such a joke. It's as good a theory as anyone else's.

Ruth   It's not the *theory* that people will find funny sweetie.

It's the idea of showing Madame your. *Little animals.*

That's what's hilarious.

Oh and it's not just me.

Kathy here finds your drawings a complete hoot too.

Tommy looks at Kathy.

We were having a good laugh about them the other day.

Tommy looks at Kathy.

Laughing at all those stupid combinations you've drawn.

We were in complete hysterics about them.

Weren't we Kathy?

Tommy looks at Kathy.

Kathy doesn't speak.

Doesn't speak.

Tommy walks away.

Kathy is about to call out to him. But stops herself.

He's gone.

Kathy looks at Ruth. Then turns and walks away.

What's your problem now?

Kathy   You Ruth. You're my problem.

Ruth Oh here we go –

Kathy You're bloody awful you know that? You must know it! The way you act. The stuff you do –

Ruth It's not my fault you're too much of a coward to stand up for yourself!

Kathy You make everyone's lives miserable Ruth –

Ruth Well at least I don't act like I'm superior to everyone! At first I thought you were just shy. But the real reason you don't talk to anyone is because you actually think you're something special.

Well you're not special Kathy.

You're ordinary.

On the word 'ordinary' there's a low, almost imperceptible hum.

So ordinary no one can bring themselves to be with you.

The hum *gets louder.*

Ruth turns and walks away.

Kathy I wanted you to know.

I've arranged it with Keffers.

I'm starting my training early.

Ruth stops.

I'm leaving the Cottages Ruth.

I'm leaving to become a carer.

Ruth remains with her back to Kathy. Her fists clenched. Her breathing shallow.

Ruth Good for you Kathy.

The hum *gets louder.*
You're clearly not fitting in here.
So it's best for us all that you go.
Ruth exits.
Kathy holds her chest.
The hum *gets louder and louder.*
The lights get brighter and brighter.
Emotion exploding within her.
End of Act One.

Act Two

SCENE ONE: A RECEPTION AREA

Kathy sits. Reading a book. A small suitcase with her.

A few chairs down another donor, Jessica, sits. A backpack by her side.

Kathy reads.

A projection appears: '1998'.

Jessica looks around the space.

Checks her watch.

Looks around.

Jessica Are these your final checks before admission?

Kathy looks up. Nods.

I was supposed to be in an hour ago.

Kathy They often run late.

Kathy smiles.

Goes back to her book.

Jessica I hope my friends come to visit me.

I'm the first of my lot to become a donor and.

I hope they come to see how I'm doing.

Kathy I'm sure they will.

Jessica Thanks.

I'm sure your friends will come too.

A low, almost imperceptible hum.

Kathy smiles.

Closes the book.

Stands.

Are you leaving?

Kathy Just going to stretch my legs.

They'll be on their lunch break now. Nothing will happen until they're back.

Jessica Where are you going?

Kathy There's a little stretch of beach near here.

Kathy is instantly on the beach.

Jessica disappears.

I like looking out at it.

The hum *gets louder.*

The sea.

Kathy closes her eyes.

The hum *gets louder.*

The lights get brighter.

Louder.

Brighter.

Louder.

The sound and light suddenly stop.

Laura Kathy?

SCENE TWO: A CAR PARK

Laura Kathy H!

Kathy turns to see Laura (twenty-five).

Kathy Laura?!

A projection appears: 'PART THREE: 1992'.

Laura I was walking past and I thought. That looks just like Kathy H.

And it was you!

They embrace.

You look great.

Kathy Thanks.

Laura Blimey. I haven't seen you since you left the Cottages.

Kathy No I suppose that's right.

Laura I heard you're doing really well.

Kathy H the brilliant carer who's in high demand.

Kathy Oh well I don't know about that.

Laura How long have you been doing it now?

Kathy About five years.

Laura Five? Bloody hell. And you're still going strong.

I can't stand it. Being a carer. I can't wait to stop doing it.

Kathy I'm sure your donors would be sad if you stopped.

Laura I'm sure they wouldn't.

I've got this one who's such a bloody pain. Irritable with me all the time. Nothing I do is good enough and he's at that centre in Worthing. Do you know that one?

Kathy indicates no.

The whitecoats there are just awful. There's one in particular who has it in for me and I just feel so alone with it all and it's really good to see you Kathy did I say that already?

Kathy It's good seeing you too Laura.

Laura Sorry I'm a bit.

One of my donors completed this morning and it wouldn't normally get to me but she was only on her second and.

There were. Unexpected complications.

Kathy Well you can't let it get you down.

Laura No. No.

You've got to keep going haven't you?

Kathy Have you bumped into any of the old gang?

Laura Not really.

It's funny. I thought we'd run into each all the time.

I saw Alfie D about a year ago. He seemed to be doing okay.

And I saw Ruth a few months back.

Kathy Oh really?

How was she?

Laura Okay. She'd just been given notice for her first donation.

	It was a bit awkward actually.
	We hadn't parted the best of friends back at the Cottages.
Kathy	I didn't realise you'd fallen out.
Laura	It wasn't a big deal. You remember what she was like.
	If anything she got worse after you left. Always telling everyone what to do.
	Have you seen her?
Kathy	No.
Laura	You know. I heard a rumour.
	That her first donation was really bad.
Kathy	I heard that too.
Laura	Poor Ruth.

Laura looks at the ground.

Kathy looks at the ground.

I also heard she's had trouble with her carers. They've had to change them around a lot for her.

Kathy Not surprising really. Can you imagine?

Being Ruth's carer.

Laura laughs.

Kathy laughs.

Laura I hate being a carer.

All I want is for them to give me my notice so I can stop doing it.

Now that most of our lot are. Getting on with it.

I don't want to get left behind.

	Anyway.
	I better be going.
Kathy	It was lovely seeing you Laura.
Laura	It's weird isn't it? Thinking it's all gone.
Kathy	What's gone?
Laura	Oh Kath don't you know?
	Hailsham.
	It's closed down.
Kathy	What?
Laura	Apparently they sold the grounds to this hotel chain or something.
Kathy	But what about the students?
Laura	I suppose they've been transferred to other places.
	Laura walks away.
Kathy	No I didn't mean the students now.
	Laura keeps walking. Kathy calls out –
	I meant us.
	Laura is gone.
	What about all of us?
Ruth	Is that a joke?

SCENE THREE: A ROOM

Kathy No. You are looking better.

Better than last time.

Ruth is sitting up in bed wearing pyjamas. She's attached to a drip. Kathy standing opposite.

You probably don't remember my last visit. You were in and out for most of it.

Kathy rummages in a shopping bag. Pulls out a bottle of water and a packet of biscuits. Puts them on the table.

(*Pointing to the biscuits.*) They're the right ones aren't they?

Ruth Yes.

They're the right ones.

You look nice.

I like your hair.

Kathy Thank you.

Do you want a glass? For the –

Ruth Why did you ask to be my carer?

You did ask didn't you?

That's what they told me.

Kathy Would you rather I wasn't?

Ruth That's not what I'm saying.

Kathy Because I could get them to change it if you –

Ruth I just wanted to know why that's all.

Kathy So I could help you.

Ruth	Why would you want to do that?
Kathy	Why do you think?
	They look at one another.
	Look.
Ruth	Could you open the blind?
	Kathy opens the blind. Light comes streaming in.
	The view is of the rooftops of Dover. The sea in the distance.
	Kathy looks at the view.
	You heard then. That I had a bad first donation.
Kathy	Yes.
Ruth	Do you feel sorry for me?
	Ruth the terrible donor.
Kathy	No –
Ruth	Can't even get through her first properly.
Kathy	No.
Ruth	Then why are you here?
	Why bother coming after all this time?
Kathy	Alright.
	Maybe I did feel a bit bad for you when I first heard.
	But seeing you now.
	Seeing how you're still so.
	Defiant.
	I can assure you I'm not feeling sorry for you one little bit.

Ruth	Good.

Ruth turns to a small drawer next to the bed. Tries to open it.

Stops in pain.

Kathy goes to the drawer. Opens it.

There's an envelope in there.

Kathy takes out a large envelope.

Open it.

Kathy does. She starts to read a letter.

It's from Hannah.

She sent them on.

Apparently she found them among some of her old things.

Kathy looks at the enclosed pages.

Kathy	Your boats!
Ruth	Silly really. But she wanted me to have them.
Kathy	They're wonderful aren't they?

Ruth suppresses a smile.

Do you want me to put them up?

Ruth shrugs.

Kathy takes some tape out of the drawer and sticks the paintings on the wall next to the bed.

They're childlike paintings of sailboats on the water. Each with different-coloured sails.

Ruth	Hannah says they were the most expensive thing she ever bought at the Exchanges.
Kathy	You charged four tokens for them.

Ruth	No I didn't. I would never have charged four.
Kathy	You said if people wanted quality they had to pay.
Ruth	God. What a madam I was.
	Still.
	It was quite the bargain looking at them now.
	Kathy and Ruth look at the paintings.
	They look at them.
	You don't have to be my carer Kathy.
Kathy	I know.
Ruth	I mean.
	You don't have to feel obliged.
Kathy	I don't Ruth. Really.
	But it's nice for me too. Having donors that I know and that I.
	It's nice for me.
	Kathy looks out at the view.
	It's lovely here.
Ruth	It's alright I suppose.
Kathy	I've seen a lot of recovery centres. And this one's so clean and.
	Comfortable. You even have a balcony.
	With a view of the sea.
	I'd like to get placed somewhere like this.
	Kathy and Ruth look out.
	They look.

Ruth	I wish I'd kept my collection of things from the Exchanges.
Kathy	What did you do with them?
Ruth	When I went to the Cottages. All my precious items were packed into a box. Patricia's watercolours. Christy's book of poems.

One of Marjorie P's giraffes. |
| Kathy | Oh Marjorie's giraffes! |
| Ruth | I thought I'd find a really good wooden chest for it all and keep it in there.

But when I saw that none of the veterans had collections.

It was only us.

I didn't find a wooden chest.

I just stuffed everything into a bin bag and threw it all away. |
| Kathy | Ruth you didn't? |
| Ruth | I told Keffers to take it to a charity shop. But he just laughed. Said no one would want any of it. I kept telling him it was really good stuff. He humoured me in the end. Said he'd try. But he obviously just tossed it all in the bin.

I wish I'd kept it now of course.

It would be lovely to look at it all and.

Remember.

I like thinking back on Hailsham. Especially the early stuff. |
| Kathy | I try to forget it. |
| Ruth | Why would you want to forget it? |

Kathy	I don't know.
	Something about the past just feels.
	Sad.
	Ruth looks away.
Ruth	You were always much stronger than me.
Kathy	I most certainly wasn't Ruth. You were a force.
Ruth	But you didn't care. How others saw you.
	For me that was.
	It was what I cared about most.
	Ruth looks at her boat paintings.
	I wish I'd kept it now of course.
	I wish I'd kept it.
Kathy	(*Reading.*) 'Art is the nearest thing to life . . .'

SCENE FOUR: A BALCONY

The sun is setting as Kathy and Ruth sit on the balcony of Ruth's room. Kathy reads from a book. Ruth sits with her eyes closed. She is in a dressing gown. The drip no longer attached.

Kathy	'It is a mode of amplifying experience and extending our contact with our fellow men beyond the bounds of our personal lot.'
	Kathy looks up. She sees Ruth's eyes are closed.
	She closes the book quietly.
Ruth	(*Eyes closed.*) Don't stop.
Kathy	Oh. I thought you were sleeping.

Ruth	No. I was just.
	Resting my eyes.
	Ruth opens her eyes. Sits up.
	Although I'm a bit lost. You might need to take it back.
Kathy	To which part?
Ruth	I don't know.
Kathy	We can come back to it later.
Ruth	I was never very good with literature.
	You were always much more. Bookish than me.
Kathy	Thanks a lot.
Ruth	It's not a bad thing.
Kathy	It doesn't sound like a good thing.
Ruth	Don't be silly. I would have loved to have been as clever as you.
	Ruth drinks her tea.
	Kathy looks out at the view.
	I still can't believe Hailsham's closed.
Kathy	Me neither.
Ruth	It's all gone. Just like that.
	I heard it was being turned into flats.
Kathy	Laura said something about a hotel chain.
Ruth	I always thought I'd go back there one day.
	See it again.
	Kathy looks down at the book.
	Do you remember that pencil case I had?

Kathy Yes.

Ruth I was trying to think of all the things I'd got from the Sales. And that pencil case suddenly came to mind.

Now that was something wasn't it?

Kathy It really was.

You told everyone it was a present from the guardians.

Ruth Did I?

Kathy Yes. You said it was a secret present they gave you for being so special.

Ruth Well that was bloody stupid of me.

Kathy I never believed it for a second.

Ruth I loved the Sales.

Kathy So did I.

Ruth Where do you think they got it all from? That stuff.

Kathy Who knows. Most of it was broken rubbish.

Ruth Oh but there were some real gems.

Kathy Yes.

Like my tape.

Ruth's smile drops.

She looks down at her hands.

Down at her hands.

Kathy suddenly stands and Ruth lets out a sound of vocalised shock, as she holds up her arms to defend herself.

	I was just going to get my scarf.
Ruth	Sorry you.
	Shocked me. When you stood up like that it just. I was.
	Shocked.
Kathy	I'm not going to hurt you Ruth.

Ruth looks away. Lowers her arms.

| Ruth | I just wasn't expecting it. You standing suddenly like that. |

Ruth looks away.

Kathy looks at Ruth.

Kathy	Do you think this is working?
	Me being your carer?
Ruth	What makes you say that?
Kathy	Because you don't seem very.
	This doesn't seem very.
	Relaxed.
	And it's important for you. During this time that you –
Ruth	No I don't want you to say that don't say that.
Kathy	Okay.
	I'm just going to get my scarf.

Kathy exits leaving Ruth alone on the balcony.

Ruth shakes her head to herself.

| Ruth | (*Quietly.*) Stupid stupid stupid. |

Ruth picks up her tea.

Her hands are shaking.

She puts the mug down. Sits on her hands.

Kathy enters wrapping the scarf around her neck.

Kathy   It's beautiful out here.

Just a bit chilly.

You're not too cold are you?

Ruth   I'm fine.

Kathy   Okay well just say if you are and we'll go back in.

Kathy sits. Takes a biscuit. Eats.

Ruth watches her.

Ruth   There's a donor here on the next floor. Charlotte. She was telling me about this boat near the Kingsfield Centre?

It's this little fishing boat. With a small cabin.

And it's just sitting there apparently.

Stranded in the marshes.

Kathy   How did it get there?

Ruth   How do I know? Maybe they wanted to dump it. Whoever owned it.

Or maybe when everything got flooded it just drifted in and got itself beached.

She said it's really beautiful.

Her carer took her to see it.

Kathy   And it's by the Kingsfield Centre?

Ruth	Yes. It's just off the road she said so it's easy enough to get to.
Kathy	That's not particularly close you know.
	The Kingsfield Centre.
Ruth	No I know.
	I was just saying.
	I'm not suggesting anything.
	Kathy looks at the book.
	Looks up at Ruth.
Kathy	But you'd like to see it?
	If I could find a time.
	You'd like to go and see this boat?
Ruth	Yes I suppose I would.
	You spend day after day in a place like this. Yes.
	It would be nice to see something like that.
Kathy	And if we did go.
	If we did drive all that way.
	Would you want to visit Tommy?
	Seeing as he's at the Kingsfield Centre too.
Ruth	That wasn't the only reason I was bringing up the boat.
	I really do want to see it. You spend all this time in and out of hospital. Cooped up in here and you hear about something like that and you feel this sort of. Yearning to see it.
	It's hard to explain. But those kind of things mean more than they once did.

	But yes. Okay.
	I did know Tommy was at the Kingsfield Centre.
Kathy	And you want to see Tommy?
Ruth	(*Without hesitation.*) Yes.
	Yes I do.
	I haven't seen that boy for a long time.
Kathy	How did things end between you?
Ruth	Pretty uneventfully really.
	After you left the Cottages. We more or less drifted apart.
	We never fought or anything. But there was something. Missing.
	Like the glue that was keeping us together was no longer there.
	But we never ended things officially. Since we were both going to different places for our training it didn't seem worth it. So we stayed together until I left.
	We've not seen each other since.
	But it's not just about Tommy.
	I really do want to see that boat too.
	The sound of traffic passing.

SCENE FIVE: A CAR

Kathy in the driver's seat. Ruth, dressed, sitting next to her.

Kathy drives. Ruth looks out.

Ruth turns on the radio. News and music stations fade in and out between white noise.

Ruth turns off the radio.

Ruth He definitely knows we're coming?

Kathy He should do.

I sent a note to his carer saying we were passing this afternoon. And if he didn't want us to stop by. To let me know.

And I've heard nothing so.

He must be okay with it.

Ruth takes a breath. Clenches her jaw.

How are you feeling?

Ruth Fine. A little achy in the back but other than that. Fine.

Kathy I didn't mean physically.

Ruth Fine.

I wonder if he looks the same.

How many donations has he had?

Kathy Two I believe.

Apparently he did well in both though.

Ruth Yes I can imagine that. He was always so fit wasn't he?

Always running around and things.

Kathy rounds a corner.

Kathy   Oh look. There's a group of people over there. Maybe he's with them.

Kathy stops the car.

Ruth   What do we do what do we do what do we do?

Kathy   Well I suppose we go and say hello.

Ruth   No we should stay here let's just stay here I want to stay.

Kathy   Come on Ruth. We've come all this way.

Kathy unclips her seatbelt and gets out of the car.

Ruth remains inside.

As Kathy steps out, a group of donors appear, standing together.

Hello?

They stop talking and look up. One of the group turns around.

Tommy.

Tommy approaches Kathy and they stand looking at one another.

Tommy smiles.

Kathy smiles.

They embrace.

Ruth watches from the car. Her expression still.

Tommy   It's good to see you Kath.

You haven't changed a bit.

Kathy   Good to see you too Tommy.

They look at one another.

Look.

Ruth's in the car.

Tommy walks to the car. Gets in through the back passenger door.

Kathy stands outside the car. Giving them a moment. Tommy kisses Ruth on the cheek in greeting and they talk to one another. Their conversation muted.

Ruth smiles as she talks to Tommy.

After a moment Kathy approaches the car and opens the driver's door. As she does Ruth and Tommy's dialogue becomes instantly audible.

Tommy   . . . what I heard too.

It's been stranded there for a few months I think.

Kathy   Are you talking about this boat?

Tommy   Yeah everyone here's been talking about it.

I nearly went to see it a while ago but I couldn't go in the end because I had some bleeding.

That was ages ago though. I don't get anything like that any more.

How about you Ruth? How are you feeling?

Ruth   Fine thanks.

Fine.

Ruth's gaze is entirely fixed on Tommy.

Better for seeing you Tommy.

Tommy half smiles.

Tommy Should we get going?

Kathy Yes!

Now from what I can see we should get there in about –

The sound of wind and water.

SCENE SIX: MARSHLAND

Kathy, Ruth and Tommy sit on the sand as they look out.

Ruth It's beautiful.

The unseen boat beached in the distance ahead.

Kathy Yes.

They look out to the boat.

It really is.

Tommy When I imagine Hailsham now. I see it as being like this.

Ruth Isn't Hailsham a hotel or something?

Tommy No I know it's just. When I think of it.

Without the students.

This is pretty close to the picture in my head.

Except there's no boat of course.

Kathy Do you think about Hailsham a lot Tommy?

Tommy All the time.

Ruth Me and Kath we always talk about it. Don't we?

Remembering things.

Tommy	You know Simon P was at my centre for a while. He's left now. Gone up north somewhere for his third donation.
	I never heard how he got on.
	Have either of you heard?
	Kathy and Ruth indicate no.
Ruth	I did hear about Chrissie though.
	Heard she completed during her second.
Tommy	Yes I heard that too. It must be right. I heard exactly the same.
	Shame.
	Only her second as well.
	Glad that didn't happen to me.
Ruth	I think it probably happens much more than they ever tell us.
	My carer over there. She probably knows that's right but she won't say.
Kathy	There's no big conspiracy about it. Sometimes it happens.
Ruth	I bet it happens much more than they tell us.
Kathy	I ran into Rodney a while ago. He was in a centre in York.
	He was doing okay.
Ruth	I bet he was devastated about Chrissie.
Kathy	Actually he wasn't too bad about it. He was sad obviously. But they hadn't seen each other for a couple of years.
	Said he thought Chrissie wouldn't have minded too much.

Ruth	How on earth could he know that? How could he possibly know what Chrissie was feeling?
Kathy	I'm only telling you what he said.
Ruth	He wasn't the one lying on the table clinging for life. I bet he was really devastated about Chrissie. I bet he was but he was just pretending to be okay about it.
Kathy	Well he didn't seem that devastated.
Ruth	You have no idea what any of it feels like Kathy. You're still a carer. You've got no idea.
Kathy	I get to see a lot as a carer.
Ruth	But you've no idea what it's really like.
Kathy	Alright Ruth. No need to get upset.
Ruth	Well it's ridiculous. Claiming to know what people are feeling when you haven't got a clue.
Tommy	I don't think Kath was claiming anything Ruth. She was just telling us what Rodney said.
	They look out to the boat.
	Look out.
	I never really liked them. Rodney and Chrissie.
	They always seemed a bit.
	Fake or something.
Kathy	Yes.
Ruth	They weren't fake. They were just different.
Tommy	But it was like they were play-acting all the time.
	Pretending to be like those people off the telly. From that rubbish series they used to watch.

Kathy	That awful American show.
Tommy	Yeah. With all that fake laughter.
Ruth	Well I didn't mind it.
	And I didn't mind them.
Tommy	They had such a thing about us being from Hailsham. They'd go on and on about it like it made us so different or something.
Ruth	Well it did make us different Tommy. You must know that.
Kathy	I think they thought we were far more different than we really were.
	And you didn't help Ruth. All that stuff you'd spout.
	Didn't you tell Chrissie that you were going to go and work in an office?
Ruth	I can't remember.
Kathy	Chrissie would talk about it all the time. How you were going to work in an office after the Cottages.
Ruth	It was just a silly thing I probably said.
Tommy	Oh yeah. And we went to see your possible who worked in that office.
Kathy	And Chrissie said it was just like the office you were going to work in.
Ruth	Well she wasn't my possible in the end. Was she.
Kathy	Don't you ever think though. Maybe you should have tried?
Ruth	Tried what?

Kathy	Working in an office.
Ruth	What are you talking about? How could I have tried?
Kathy	I don't know. I mean you'd have been the first. Doing something like that.
	But you talked about it so much. You could have at least tried.
Ruth	It's just something I used to dream about is all.
Kathy	But if you were so sure that you weren't.
	Ordinary.
	Like the rest of us.
	You should have at least given it a go.
Tommy	Yes Kathy's right. You might as well have looked into it.
Ruth	How? Where would I have gone?
	There wasn't a way to look into it.
Kathy	I don't know.
	You could have gone back to Hailsham and asked.
	And even if it hadn't worked.
	Even if they'd have said no. At least you'd be sitting here now.
	Knowing that you tried.
Ruth	Kathy.
	I don't expect you to forgive me.
	But I'm going to ask you to all the same.
	Kathy looks out at the boat.

Looks at the boat.

I want to go now.

Tommy will you help me up? I want to go.

Tommy stands, holding out an arm to help Ruth up.

Kathy remains looking at the boat.

Kathy let's go.

I want to go.

Kathy Forgive you for what Ruth?

Ruth Forgive me for what?

Ruth laughs.

Is that a joke?

Well for starters there's the times I lied to you about your urges.

I knew how worried you were about it and I should have told you. I should have told you how it was exactly the same for me too. Just the way you described it.

And I should have told you how even though I was with Tommy I couldn't resist doing it with other people. At least three others while we were at the Cottages and I know there's no reason for you to forgive me for that but I want to ask you because.

Ruth stops.

Kathy Because what?

Ruth Because nothing.

Anyway that's not the half of it. Not even a small bit of it actually. The main thing is.

The main thing.

Is that I kept you and Tommy apart.

Ruth looks at Tommy.

That was the worst thing I did.

And I'm not expecting you to forgive me.

God I've said this in my head so many times I can't believe I'm really doing it.

It should have been you two. I'm not pretending I didn't always see that. Of course I did. As far back as I can remember. But I kept you apart.

I'm not expecting you to forgive me. That's not what I'm after just now.

What I want is for you to put it right.

Put right what I messed up for you.

Tommy How do you mean Ruth? How do you mean put it right?

Kathy covers her face.

She breaks.

Breaks.

Ruth Kathy listen.

You and Tommy. You've got to try and get a deferral.

If it's you two there's a chance. A real chance.

Kathy It's too late for that. It's far too late.

Ruth It's not too late Kathy. Listen to me.

It's not too late.

	Okay so Tommy's done two donations. But who's to say that has to make a difference?
Kathy	It's too late for all that now.
	It's stupid even thinking about it. As stupid as wanting to work in that office.
	We're all beyond that now.
Ruth	It's not too late Kathy.
	Tommy you tell her.
	Listen both of you.
	I wanted us all to do this trip because I wanted to say what I just said.
	But also. Because I wanted to give you something.

Ruth rummages around in her pockets. Pulls out a crumpled piece of paper.

Tommy you'd better take this. Look after it.

Then when Kathy changes her mind you'll have it.

Tommy	What is it?
Ruth	It's Madame's address.

Tommy takes the paper.

Tommy	How did you find this?
Ruth	It wasn't easy. It took me a long time and I ran a few risks.
	But I got it in the end. And I got it for you.
	Both of you.
	Now it's up to you to find her and try.

It's like you were saying to me Kathy.

You've at least got to try.

Kathy and Tommy look at Ruth.

Tommy disappears.

Kathy looks at Ruth.

Looks.

Will you keep my boat paintings?

SCENE SEVEN: A ROOM

Kathy Oh be quiet will you.

Ruth is sitting up in bed wearing a hospital gown.

Kathy standing next to her.

Ruth You better not throw them in the bin.

Kathy I'm serious Ruth. I won't have that talk do you hear?

Ruth looks to the window.

Ruth It is lovely here now I think about it.

Kathy looks to the window.

Kathy It really is.

Ruth Have you thought any more about becoming Tommy's carer?

Kathy As I keep telling you. It's not as easy as all that.

People seem to assume I can pick and choose my donors willy-nilly.

Ruth Think about it Kath will you?

Please.

Think about it.

Kathy looks at Ruth.

Kathy · You know what I was thinking about?

I don't know why but it just came to mind.

Those sex talks we used to get from Miss Emily.

Ruth laughs.

Do you remember?

Ruth · (*As Miss Emily.*) The penis enters the vagina. Here.

Kathy laughs.

They were absolutely hysterical.

Kathy · None of us found them funny at the time.

Ruth · We were too shocked.

Kathy · Too traumatised more like.

Ruth · She must have been quite the goer in her day.

Kathy laughs.

Ruth laughs.

I mean she knew things no book could teach.

They laugh.

Silent laughter.

Laugh until their stomachs ache.

Porter · Ruth C?

Two Porters enter the room.

They wheel Ruth's bed towards the exit.

Ruth holds out her arm behind her.

>   *Kathy squeezes Ruth's hand.*
>   *Ruth and the Porters are gone.*
>   *Kathy looks to the door.*
>   *Looks.*

Kathy Surely I can see her now?

SCENE EIGHT: A HALLWAY

Nurse There were.

Unexpected complications.

Kathy But it's been two days.

Nurse Let me go and check.

The Nurse exits.

Kathy takes a breath.

Closes her eyes.

You can go in.

Kathy walks to the door.

But you should know she's very close. To completing.

Kathy steps into the room.

The sound of hospital machinery beeping.

Ruth lies on the bed. Tubes attached to her.

Kathy Ruth. It's me.

It's Kath.

Ruth opens her eyes.

Blinks slowly. As if taking great effort.

You're doing alright Ruth.

They said you're doing alright.

Ruth closes her eyes.

I'm really glad I became your carer.

Even though you're a bit of a madam.

Kathy smiles.

Ruth makes a sound.

It's alright.

I'm here.

I'm here.

And I want you to know.

I'm going to do it Ruth.

I'm going to become Tommy's carer.

I'm going to do it.

As soon as I can.

Ruth takes Kathy's hand.

Squeezes it.

The beeping slows.

Slows.

Stops.

Ruth disappears.

Kathy remains.

Remains.

Remains.

Tommy Let's see then Kath.

SCENE NINE: A ROOM

Kathy and Tommy are sitting in Tommy's room.

Tommy   Let's see if you got it right.

Kathy   I'm going to say I'm feeling pretty confident Tommy.

Tommy   Come on then.

   What you get?

   Kathy pulls each item out of a carrier bag as she announces it.

Kathy   Football magazine.

   Wotsits.

   Ribena.

   Tommy laughs.

Tommy   Spot on Kathy. That's spot on!

   No wonder you're such a good carer.

Kathy   Well I had something of an advantage.

Tommy   I suppose you do know me better than anyone.

   Tommy smiles.

   Kathy smiles.

   I just can't believe I'm going to see you all the time.

Kathy   You're going to be sick of me by the end.

Tommy   That's not possible Kath.

   I'll never be sick of you.

Kathy   I'll remind you of that in six months.

   Tommy laughs.

He takes Kathy's hand.

Kathy looks at their hands.

She looks up at Tommy.

Tommy pulls Kath towards him.

They kiss.

Kiss.

Kiss.

They laugh.

Tommy You know Kath.

I've been doing my drawings again.

Ever since that day at the boat. I started them again.

I've got books and books of them. And I think some of them are really good.

Do you think we should try Kath?

With this deferral business?

Kathy I don't know Tommy.

You've got your third coming up.

Tommy That gives us all the more reason.

Assuming I'll be okay after my third.

And I'm sure I will I mean. Look at me.

I'm in pretty good shape. Even if I do say so myself.

Kathy You're in very good shape Tommy.

Tommy Well then. That time after my third. That's when we have to try.

	No one makes it after their fourth. We both know that.
	And I think we'd have a really good chance with these deferrals. I really do.
Kathy	But what if we don't have a good enough chance?
	That's what scares me Tommy. The idea of getting nothing. That terrifies me.
Tommy	Then at least we tried.
	And it's got to be worth a try hasn't it Kath?
	A deferral for three or four years.
	That's got to be worth a try.
	Kathy leans over and kisses Tommy.
	He kisses her back.
	Kathy looks at Tommy.
	Smiles.
Kathy	I'm sorry. We didn't mean to shock you.

SCENE TEN: A DOORWAY

Kathy and Tommy, holding a large bag, stand opposite Madame in her doorway.

Madame	What are you doing here?
Tommy	We were at Hailsham.
Kathy	Kathy H and Tommy D.
Madame	I don't understand.
Tommy	We wanted to talk to you about something.
	Something very important.

	And we brought some things to show you.
Madame	There's nothing I want from you.
Kathy	Well they're not for you exactly.
Tommy	They're for your gallery.
Madame	My *gallery?*

Madame looks at them both.

You better come in.

Madame opens the door and indicates for them to enter –

SCENE ELEVEN: A DRAWING ROOM

The room is dark. The curtains drawn. The sound of a clock ticking.

Madame Wait here.

And don't touch anything.

Madame exits.

Kathy and Tommy stand alone in the room. They look around the space.

Tommy Good old Ruth.

She really did find her.

Kathy She did.

Tommy points to a painting on the wall.

Tommy Look. It's a painting of Hailsham.

They look at the painting.

That's the bit round the back of the playing field.

Kathy Oh yeah. There's the duck pond.

They look at the painting.

I'm really nervous.

Tommy It's okay.

We're going to be okay.

Voice Well isn't this quite the surprise?

Kathy and Tommy turn. The voice coming from the darkness.

A wheelchair emerges from the darkness, being pushed by Madame.

Tommy Miss Emily?

In it sits Miss Emily. Frail. Contorted.

Miss Emily Quite the surprise indeed.

Look at the two of you. You look very well. Very well indeed.

Now what were your names?

Madame goes to speak.

No don't tell me Marie-Claude! I want to remember.

You're the boy with the bad temper. The bad temper but a big heart.

Tommy D.

And you of course are Kathy H. We've heard a lot about you and how well you've done as a carer.

I remember you see. I dare say I can remember you all.

Kathy It's very good to see you Miss Emily.

Miss Emily Well it cheers me no end to see you too. And I believe it cheers Marie-Claude. Even though you'd never know it to look at her.

Madame looks at Kathy and Tommy. An expression of trepidation on her face.

You could try to look a little less formidable darling.

Madame's expression doesn't change. Miss Emily looks to Tommy and Kathy.

So what is it that brings you here? Marie-Claude said you've brought something for us.

Tommy Well I'm not sure if you remember Miss Emily.

But when I was at Hailsham. I wasn't very good at being creative.

To be honest I sort of gave up with it all. So none of my things were ever selected for the Gallery.

Which is why I wanted to bring you these.

Tommy takes his notebooks out of his bag.

My drawings. I've been working really hard on them.

And they should give you what you need.

He holds the drawing books out to Miss Emily.

Miss Emily doesn't take the books, so Tommy starts showing her the work himself.

I've got about ten full books here. There's more at the centre. But these show my best work I think.

Miss Emily And why do you think we need to see your artwork Tommy?

Tommy Because our artwork shows who we are.

Inside.

Miss Emily It shows your soul is that what you mean?

Tommy Exactly.

Miss Emily And why would we need to see your soul Tommy?

Tommy So you can see if Kath and I are truly.

Properly.

In love.

Miss Emily I see.

So this is about the deferrals.

Tommy Yes!

Kathy We're here to see if we qualify for a deferral.

Madame I told you –

Miss Emily holds her hand up to stop her.

Miss Emily Let them finish Marie-Claude.

Tommy I know I've started my donations. But we've only just found each other again.

Me and Kath.

And we really do think.

We believe.

That we qualify.

Don't we Kath?

Kathy We do.

We really do.

Tommy holds out his artwork to Miss Emily.

Miss Emily I don't need to see your art to know you're in love Tommy. That's quite clear just from looking at you both.

Seeing how much time and thought you've put into coming here today shows me that you are very well matched indeed.

When Hailsham was still open we used to get two or three couples a year coming to us asking for a deferral. Didn't we Marie-Claude?

Madame Sometimes more.

Miss Emily But you're the first in quite some time.

I used to wonder how this story continued to exist year after year. Even after we tried to stamp it out.

And after many years of hearing it I began to think perhaps I shouldn't worry. It's not my doing after all. And for the few couples who get disappointed the rest will never put it to the test anyway.

It's something for them to dream about. A little fantasy.

Something to give them hope.

But for the two of you I can see this doesn't apply. You're serious. You've thought carefully. You've *hoped* carefully.

And that makes me feel genuine regret.

Tommy I don't understand.

Do we qualify or not?

Kathy   Miss Emily's saying the deferrals aren't real Tommy.

Miss Emily   I'm very sorry. I really am.

Tommy   But if the deferrals don't exist. Then why did you take all our art away? What was the point of the Gallery?

Miss Emily   The Gallery? Well that rumour *did* have some truth to it.

You were right about one thing Tommy. Your art was used to reveal what you were like *inside*.

We took your art to show people your souls. Or to put it more finely.

We did it to prove you *had* souls.

Kathy   Why would you have to prove a thing like that?

Miss Emily   It's touching that you're so shocked by this Kathy.

When Marie-Claude and I started Hailsham we wanted to show the world that if donors were reared in humane cultivated environments it was possible for them to grow to be as sensitive and intelligent as any ordinary human being.

Before that. All clones.

Or *students* as we preferred to call you.

Existed only to supply medical science.

And most people didn't believe you had souls at all.

They still don't.

That's why we collected your work. Had special exhibitions showing the best of it. 'There look!'

	we'd say. 'Look at their art! How dare you claim these children are anything less than fully human?'
Kathy	But why would people want to believe otherwise?
Miss Emily	Because no one wants to confront the reality of who you are. When you're the reason they're no longer dying of cancer. Motor neurone disease. Heart failure. It suits them for you to be other.
	Different.
	Less than human.
	Because if your lives don't matter. Then it doesn't matter what you're being made to do.
	Marie-Claude and I started Hailsham to prove otherwise. And we began to make progress. We could see a real shift in feeling.
	But all it took was another health crisis for people to become afraid again. And wanting all of you to go back into the shadows.
	You won't find anything like Hailsham now. All you'll find are those terrible government 'homes'. And let me tell you my dears. You'd not sleep for days if you saw what goes on in some of those places.
Tommy	So there's absolutely no deferral?
Kathy	Tommy.
Miss Emily	No Tommy.
	There's no deferral.
	Your life must now run the course that's been set for it.

Tommy And everything we did. All the lessons. The art. The books. It was all about proving a point to other people.

Miss Emily It might feel as though you were just pawns in a game.

But you have to understand.

You were lucky pawns.

Kathy That's why everything felt so unclear.

You didn't *want* us to know who we were.

Miss Emily What was the alternative? Drilling it into you every day of your lives?

And look at you both now! You wouldn't be who you are today if we'd not protected you. You wouldn't have lost yourselves in your art and your writing. Sport. You would have told us all that was pointless. And how could we have argued with you?

Tommy That's why Miss Lucy got so angry. She thought we needed to know more.

Miss Emily Lucy Havisham? She was a good guardian. But she wanted you to be told everything more clearly.

And we felt that wasn't in your best interest.

Kathy At least Miss Lucy liked us.

But Madame was always afraid of us. And we knew it.

Miss Emily Now you must understand. Marie-Claude has given *everything* for you. She is on your side and will always be on your side.

But of course she's afraid of you.

We're *all* afraid of you.

I had to fight back my dread of you all every day I was at Hailsham.

But I was determined not to let such feelings stop me doing what was right. I fought those feelings and I won!

Miss Emily takes a breath. Holds her chest.

Madame goes to her.

Miss Emily nods.

If you don't mind we're going to have to leave it there.

I can feel I need to lie down. I get quite tired these days you see.

But I'm so very pleased to have seen you both.

Very. Very. Pleased.

And so pleased with the way you've both turned out.

Madame wheels Miss Emily's wheelchair away. Miss Emily exits.

Tommy looks at his bag of artwork.

Kathy looks at Tommy.

Kathy   Tommy –

Tommy I don't want to talk about it.

Tommy exits.

Kathy starts to follow then –

Madame enters.

She looks at Kathy.

Madame Kathy H. Yes.

I remember.

Kathy There's something I've wanted to know for a long time.

There was a moment from Hailsham I often think about.

I was in my room listening to a song.

And I was sort of. Dancing. With my eyes closed.

And you were watching me.

You were watching. And crying. Why?

Why would you cry?

Madame I passed your dormitory and I saw you.

A little girl dancing.

Her eyes closed. Holding to her breast the old kind of world. One that she knew in her heart could not remain.

And she was holding it and pleading.

Never to let her go.

The sound of a scream.

SCENE TWELVE: A BEACH

The scream continues.

Kathy runs through the darkness, looking where it's coming from.

Kathy   Tommy.

           Tommy!

           Kathy runs into the darkness. The sound of waves crashing.

           Tommy where are you?

           Scream.

           Scream.

           Scream.

           Kathy comes upon Tommy.

           He is raging. Shouting. Flinging his fists and kicking out.

Tommy   Fucking shit fucking fuck fuck –

           Tommy falls to his knees, the tantrum continuing as he howls with grief.

           Kathy reaches out for his arms. Tries to hold him.

           He attempts to shake her off but she keeps holding on.

           Tommy's thrashing slows.

           Then stops.

           His breathing shallow.

           He starts to sob.

Her arms still around him.
He sobs as he clings hold of Kathy.
Sobs.
Sobs.
Why did they let us believe?
When it was all for nothing?

Kathy It wasn't for nothing Tommy.
We've still had some time.
And I wouldn't take that back for anything.
Tommy lets go of the embrace.
Look at you. You're covered in sand.

Tommy Oh God. I'm such an idiot.
How am I going to explain this?
We'll have to sneak in round the back.
He laughs.
I'm sorry Kath. I'm a real idiot.
Kathy sits next to Tommy.
The sound of the waves crashing.
Kath?
What are you thinking?

Kathy I was thinking about when you used to go bonkers like that at Hailsham. And we couldn't understand it. We couldn't understand how you could ever get like that.

And I was just having this idea. A thought really.

	That maybe the reason you used to get like that was because at some level.
	You *always* knew.
Tommy	I don't think so Kath.
	I think it was just me being an idiot. That's all it ever was.
	But that's a funny idea.
	Kathy touches Tommy's face. Brushes the sand away. Looks at him.
	Maybe I did know.
	Somewhere deep down.
	Maybe I did.
	Kathy looks at Tommy.
	Looks.
Kathy	Ready salted or cheese and onion?

SCENE THIRTEEN: A ROOM

Kathy and Tommy are sitting on Tommy's bed.
Kathy's holding out two bags of crisps.

Tommy	Cheese and onion.
	Kathy throws him the packet of crisps.
	They both open their packets.
	Eat their crisps.
Kathy	Once we've finished these we should get going.
	You've got your scan at three.

Tommy eats his crisps.

Maybe we could go to that boat again.

Next week. Between your checks.

See if it's still there.

What do you think?

Tommy stops eating his crisps.

Looks at the packet.

Looks.

Tommy I think I need to get a different carer.

Kathy What?

Tommy My fourth donation is coming up.

And you saw what happened last week. When I had all that kidney trouble.

There's going to be loads more stuff like that happening to me.

Kathy That's why I'm here Tommy. That's exactly why I'm here.

Tommy No.

Kathy So I could be with you for all of that.

Tommy No.

Kathy It's what Ruth wanted. Remember?

Tommy Ruth wanted that other thing for us. She wanted us to have our time together.

She wouldn't have wanted you to be my carer through this last bit.

Kathy But I'm the one who should help you.

That's why I came and found you again.

Tommy	Ruth wanted the other thing for us.
	Tommy looks at his hands.
	Looks.
	I don't want to be that way in front of you Kath.
	Ruth would have understood. She was a donor. She would have understood.
Kathy	Don't do that.
Tommy	I'm just saying. Sometimes you just don't see it. You can't see it because you're not a donor.
Kathy	You think I don't understand? I understand as well as anyone.
Tommy	It's not the same.
Kathy	I've seen more donors than any of you.
Tommy	(*Quiet.*) It's not the same.
	Aren't you tired of it? Of being a carer? The rest of us. We became donors ages ago. You've been doing it for years.
	Don't you wish they'd just hurry up and send you your notice?
Kathy	Maybe it won't be for much longer. But for now I have to keep going.
	Even if you don't want me around.
	There are others who do.
	He turns to Kathy. Holds her.
	Kathy touches Tommy's hair.
	Kisses his hair.
Tommy	I suppose you're right Kath.

You *are* a really good carer.

You'd be the perfect one for me too.

If you weren't you.

He looks out.

I keep thinking about this river somewhere. With the water moving really fast. And these two people in the water trying to hold on to each other. Holding on as hard as they can.

But in the end it's just too much. The current's too strong. They've got to let go. Drift apart.

Tommy looks at Kathy.

Kathy looks at her hands.

It's a shame Kath.

Because we've loved each other all our lives.

But in the end we can't stay together forever.

They sit in silence.

Silence.

Silence.

Kathy Are you glad Ruth completed before finding everything out?

Tommy Ruth was always different to us.

Even when we were little.

We were always trying to find things out. She wanted to believe in things the way they were. So yeah.

In a way I think it's best the way it happened.

Ruth wanted the best for us in the end.

They sit in silence.

Silence.

When I used to play football back at Hailsham. I had this thing I did.

When I scored a goal I'd go like this.

He jumps up and raises both arms in triumph.

And I'd run back to my mates with my arms up.

Like this.

His arms remain in the air as he runs back to his imaginary friends.

And in my head. When I was running back. I always imagined I was splashing through water.

Nothing deep. Just up to my ankles.

That's what I used to imagine.

Every time.

He runs as if the water is up to his ankles.

Splash splash splash.

Kathy laughs.

You've just scored. You turn. And then splash splash splash.

All this time Kath.

I never told a single soul.

Kathy laughs.

Kathy You crazy kid Tommy.

They kiss. A small kiss.

Kathy looks at Tommy.

Tommy runs as if the water is up to his ankles.

Tommy Splash splash splash.

Tommy continues running.

Kathy watches him go.

Watches him go.

Gone.

The space darkens. Kathy is the only thing illuminated.

The sound of the wind and the water.

The wind and the water.

Kathy The boat was still there.

It had sunk a little deeper.

Looked a little more battered.

But it was still there.

When I think of Hailsham.

That's how I see it too now.

I've been putting it all in order.

All the thoughts. From our time.

The memories.

I didn't want to go through them before.

It all felt too.

I don't know.

Too something.

But once I started.

Remembering.

It made me see.

Made me understand.

How lucky we were.

So lucky.

So lucky.

The sound of the wind and the water.

The wind and the water.

Hello?

SCENE FOURTEEN: A ROOM

The room is cold. Clean. Impersonal.
Kathy stands next to the bed.

Terry Oh hello.

Terry is standing in the doorway.

Sorry I was.

I didn't realise you were here.

It's Kathy isn't it?

Kathy H?

Kathy Yes.

Terry I'm Terry. Terry B.

Your carer.

Kathy Hello Terry.

Kathy lifts a duffel bag onto the bed.

Terry Was the journey long?

Kathy walks over to the window.

Kathy Not too bad.

Terry	That's good.
	Well you've got nothing on for today so you can just relax.
	Kathy pulls up the blind to reveal a beautiful sunset over the rooftops of Dover.
	You're lucky they've placed you here.
	It's one of the good ones.
Kathy	Yes.
	Yes it is.
	Kathy looks at the view.
Terry	Is there anything you'd like me to get for you?
	Newspapers?
	Magazines?
	Snacks?
Kathy	I'm alright thank you. I've just started a book. Maybe once that's finished.
Terry	Well if you're okay here I'll go and get your schedule.
Kathy	Thank you.
	Terry exits.
	Kathy starts unpacking her bag.
	She takes out some pyjamas and underwear. Sets them in the drawer.
	Takes out one of Ruth's boat paintings.
	Sticks it on the wall next to her bed.
	Takes a book out and puts it on the bedside table.

Kathy sits on the bed.

Looks at the view.

It's lovely here.

Ruth appears behind Kathy.

Ruth   It's alright I suppose.

Kathy smiles to herself.

Continues looking at the view.

Tommy   You alright there Kath?

Tommy appears behind Kathy.

Kathy remains focused on the view.

Kathy   Just thinking.

Tommy   Looks like you're thinking really hard.

Kathy turns to her bag. Takes out a Fisher-Price cassette player.

Puts the cassette player on the bedside table.

Presses play.

From the player, 'Never Let Me Go' by Judy Bridgewater plays.

Judy Bridgewater   (*Voice-over; singing.*)
Oh baby, baby . . .

Kathy stands.

She picks up the pillow from her bed as the song plays out.

She cradles the cushion in her arms.

Eyes closed.

Tommy and Ruth either side of her.

She sings along with the lyrics:

Kathy (*Singing.*)
Oh baby, baby.
Oh baby, baby.

Kathy opens her eyes.

Tommy.

Ruth.

Kathy.

Look out at us.

Look out at us.

Judy Bridgewater (*Voice-over; singing.*)
Never Let Me Go.

End of Play.